8802481 -7

799.242 Smith, Steve.
Sm6
Hunting upland
gamebirds

$16•95

DATE			

HUNTING UPLAND GAMEBIRDS

Hunting Upland Gamebirds

*What the wingshooter needs to
know about the birds, the guns,
and the new clay games*

Steve Smith

Stackpole Books

Published by
STACKPOLE BOOKS
Cameron and Kelker Streets
P.O. Box 1831
Harrisburg, PA 17105

L B

Printed in the U.S.A.

Library of Congress Cataloging-in-Publication Data

Smith, Steve.
    Hunting upland gamebirds.

    1. Upland game bird shooting.   I. Title.
SK323.S63   1987   799.2'42   87-9973
ISBN 0-8117-0871-3

For Gene Hill,
friend and teacher,
who doesn't even need to read this book.

Contents

PART I
The Birds

PART II
Guns, Gear, and Games

Foreword

Steve and I found ourselves in stuff so thick the only thing we wanted to do was get out of it. Even my little Britt, Gypsy, who'll bust brush with the best of grouse dogs, thought this was a pretty nutso place to be.

Intent on getting a look at what lay ahead, Steve crawled up on a huge rotted log. Even with the added height of the log, he was still literally up to his ears in undergrowth. With one foot on the rotted trunk and the other flogging the air, he did his best to scan the horizon.

An experienced grouse hunter would expect a grouse to take flight at a time like this, and sure enough, one did. At the roar of the flush, Steve, balanced precariously, spitting weed seeds, raised his side-by-side up and over the brush—butt plate above ear-top level—swung on the bird, and fired.

Moments later, Gypsy delivered one very dead grouse to hand. It was an absolutely incredible shot. Steve grinned.

Of such are hunting memories made, but please don't misinterpret the point: This is not to imply that the author of this book is the epitome of a great and mighty hunter, exemplary in every way, who crumples everything he shoots at. He's not, and he doesn't. When he's afield, Steve Smith wears a funny-looking hat that's been known to serve double duty as a dog dish; his pants give evidence of lost battles with barbed wire and multiflora rose, his well-worn boot soles have been burnt during attempts at rapid drying near hastily built fires. Steve's setter is usually a little overweight, a lot pampered, and, on occasion, she turns deaf. Steve slips in the mud once in a while, his nose runs when he gets cold, and, yes, he misses. I've watched the same guy who made that incredible grouse shot miss a lumbering, straightaway pheasant in a bean field at twenty-five yards—twice—over a point yet.

In other words, Steve Smith is a lot like you and me. Like him, we've made our share of incredible shots, haven't we? And missed some easy ones. We're not "Dapper Dans" in the field, we get muddy, and our noses run; our dogs are less than perfect. We like to hear leaves crackle, and campfires too. Wet dog doesn't smell all that bad, and burnt powder actually smells pretty good. We like October, maple trees with blaze orange leaves, piney hillsides, cornfields turned brown, and hunting buddies with a sense of humor. We thank God we discovered upland hunting.

If any of this makes sense to you, you'd like Steve, and I think you'll enjoy this book.

Dave Meisner
Founder, *Gun Dog* magazine

Raccoon Ridge
October 1986

Introduction

Wingshooting in North America is a sport of varied and myriad possibilities. It is a sport that draws millions, each with his perfect idea of what the sport should be. To the Texas shooter, it might be doves flighting toward water, and Our Hero is standing under a shady tree, his gun barrel heating up and his pile of spent shells attesting to the dove's deceiving speed.

To the born-and-raised Midwesterner, wingshooting is a defiant rooster pheasant, flushing at long range and cackling as he turns with the wind.

To the New Englander, ruffed grouse and woodcock in autumn splendor haunt his dreams as the dog days of summer give way to the frosty mornings when his eager setter gets him up to head for those ever-steeper hillside coverts. To the Southerner, "birds" are quail, and bobwhites at that.

This fall, I spent too much time and more money than I had

chasing doves in Mexico; pheasants and quail in Iowa; Hungarian partridge, sharptails, prairie chickens, and pheasants in South Dakota; and quail on a real Southern plantation in Georgia. In that time, I saw each of these birds at its best, because those wild things are always at their best—that's how they got there. Between those trips, there were always the ruffed grouse and woodcock of my home state of Michigan.

In each case, what drew the wingshooters to the birds was the challenge, the friendship, and the genuine love they share for the birds, the dogs, and the guns—autumn's trinity.

This book is designed to do a couple of things: to help make you a better hunter of your chosen bird; to help you better understand the bird, his habitat, and how he reacts.

It is also designed to make you a better shooter so that you can more effectively and humanely do what it is that you have come to do—shoot birds. In each section, I've tried to give you some tips on how to do things better, maybe acquire a gun you've always wanted (I didn't say "the gun" because that would imply that *one* gun is enough—HA!), or maybe understand your dog a little better.

Now you'll notice as you read that I've got some prejudices, and I hope you'll forgive me. First, I'm a hopeless double-gun fanatic. Most of what I say applies to all shooters, but a lot of it is intended for those who feel the way I do; for those who don't, this book is a blatant try to convert you.

Next, I'm a dog nut. I don't give advice about hunting without a dog because I think it's a waste of time and a waste of birds these days. As I say in one chapter, "I've got some advice for the dogless hunter: get a dog." There, I said it and I'm glad. These days, there's really no excuse for not having a dog. Many of the finest hunting breeds make good house pets during the ten months that we don't hunt but do have a dog to love and lie about. I know a lot of guys with dog hair on their good suits who will invite you outside if you tell them that a field-bred English cocker or a Brittany isn't a good house dog.

We all have our memories, about both dogs and birds. I was standing next to my car with my older son just last week after a good woodcock hunt. We were watering the dog and watching the sun go down. I pulled an empty shell from my pocket, one I'd shot a half-hour earlier, and like so many of us often do, I smelled it, savoring the burnt powder that makes your jaw muscles tighten. "Pheasants," I thought, because the smell reminded me of the cornfields and the big birds I grew up hunting back when they were around in numbers unheard of today. I handed the shell to my son and asked him to smell it and tell me what he thought of. "Woodcock" was his reply, because those are the birds of *his* youth.

That's what this book is about—it's about all of them, those birds that cackle and buzz and twitter and whirr and roar. They are difficult targets; they are worthy adversaries for a man and a dog; they are, to most of us, autumn.

Bird hunting is also about buddies. Some of these buddies are our sons, some are our fathers, because so often hunting is a family thing. Some of my buddies are insurance men and major league ballplayers, other writers and landscapers, TV technicians and ministers, retirees and kids still working on their first box of shells.

I've got a soft spot for kids. I was a teacher for a lot of years, and I still like teaching—I'm just trying a different subject with more eager students. Those of you who love the birds and the guns owe it to those youngsters—your own or someone else's—to teach them why you love hunting. They are the future; they are the ones who will have to be strong and resist the anti-hunters and the clean farmers and the chemical dumpers so that our sport, both in theory and in practice, can go on.

Now that I've told you all these things, let me tell you that I almost never take a limit of birds, because I don't need to anymore. If you do and you can, go right ahead, but let me urge you to make the transition to one who sets his own limits. Maybe three woodcock are enough, even if the law allows five; maybe six quail will do where eight or ten are legal. You know what I mean.

Wingshooting is also a year-around proposition. There are dogs to be trained, clay targets to be shot—and sporting clays, a new game in this country, is the real way to go for those of us who want to be better game shooters—and guns to be bought, traded, sold, altered, and lusted after in our hearts. Always, there are the guns. The ownership of a fine gun gives pleasure far beyond the few odd times when it goes *boom*. A fine gun is a work of art, a piece of timeless history. Those of you who own an old American or European classic gun—don't you wish it could talk, that it could tell us the places it's been, the things it's seen and done?

Guns are tools, true. But they are also time machines and escape mechanisms. Upland hunters seem to love their guns more than do those who chase other game; the gun seems to be just such a part of the sport that without that certain gun at that certain place, nothing is right.

Yet, as I hope you'll see in this book, guns are made for a job, and some guns do the job better than other guns because of the fit, balance, weight, chokes, gauge, and the shot load each can carry effectively. Each bird needs to be considered as a separate opportunity, requiring different things from a gun and the man behind the gun. The upland gun that will take quail that have flushed and scattered in an Alabama thicket is not the same gun that does the best on rooster pheasants in a South Dakota ditchrow. Both of these situations are upland shooting, but each is so different from the other that the guns we carry must reflect this difference. I hope this book tells you how to make yours that way or maybe what the best gun for the job would be.

I hope this book dispels some of the "gauge snobbery" that we have here in this country. I admit to a little of it—being a not-so-secret admirer of the 16-gauge—but for the most part, I think that maybe we in this country are not using enough gun, to paraphrase Robert Ruark a bit. We have been smitten by the light, fast 20-gauge (always, "light" and "fast" are mentioned together, although that often is not the case) to the exclusion of gauges that are more lethal in certain situations. And remember: When we pull down on a bird and have made up our minds to shoot it, we want to be lethal at that precise instant. Not sporting or gentlemanly, but lethal.

For example, if I handed you a gun that weighed, say, six pounds even, had a nice straight grip, 26-inch barrels, was bored loose improved cylinder and a light modified, and I told you it very nicely patterned one ounce of #8 shot, you'd say something like: "Aha! Sounds like a great gun for ruffed grouse!" If I then had you look it over more closely and you discovered that this fine gun happened to be a 12-gauge, would you turn up your lip, sneer at me, and brand me an infidel? If you would, then maybe your attention to gauge and not the rest of the gun's components—the more important ones—has started to get in the way.

So, that's sort of what this book is all about. I don't expect to have everyone agree with it, and maybe your experiences are different than mine. That's what makes things fun. But if you do learn something or maybe look at something a little differently, if I can help you be a better shot or a better hunter, then I've done what I set out to do. And, I had fun doing it.

PART I
The Birds

1

Doves

Dove hunting is the upland hunting situation that is most like water-fowling. I say that because a lot of the time, you're sitting down waiting for something to flap by, and, as in duck hunting, it's important to know the areas that doves are using and their flyways at any particular time.

Also, doves are migratory, like waterfowl, and subject to the vagaries of weather—doves flat out don't like cold snaps, and they'll leave the area if one blows in. Doves also test the same shooting skills that waterfowl do. Most dove hunters soon discover that there is an awful lot of air around each dove, and a lot of this air sucks in shot charges.

A lot of lousy shooting is done at doves, probably for a couple of reasons. First, they are hard to hit; they can sideslip right out of a pattern between the time you think you pull the trigger and the time the charge gets out there thirty yards. Second, the season on doves is the first to open up, and there are a lot of gung-ho—but rusty—shotgunners out there filling empty air with shotgun patterns. Also, dove hunting seems to bring out the competitive nature in hunters, and since many dove hunters may be hunting the same field, they start to press and take shots they wouldn't otherwise take in an attempt to beat the other guys. This makes for bad shooting.

Mourning doves are among nature's dumbest birds. They are lousy nesters, indifferent parents, and fragile in the face of weather and predators. But there are a lot of them—millions of them—and their numbers hold up well. Shooting has no effect on their population whatsoever. Period.

Doves eat a lot, spilled grain and weed seeds mainly, and they fly to water morning and evening. Hunting a waterhole where doves hover like miniature helicopters is pure slaughter and not very good sport. Hunting them as they fly into or away from feeding areas in grain fields is the closest thing to driven-bird shooting this continent regularly manages.

So, the smart dove hunter will find a field the birds are using, often a recently harvested field of milo, soybeans, or sweet corn (yes, doves feed on missed sweet corn like you wouldn't believe), and determine which way the birds are coming in for their morning or evening feed. Then, the hunter sets up under a flyway and takes his pokes on the pass, trying to lead the doves by enough to be successful and failing about four times out of five.

The limits on doves are usually liberal. Eight to twelve birds a day is the norm, and this limit is tough to come by. Certain areas of the country, especially the South, have strong dove-hunting traditions, and opening day is like Mardi Gras and a massive family reunion all at once. People gather in droves, there are cookouts and barbecues, and there is the dove shooting.

Also like waterfowling, dove hunting is a sport of concealment. The shooter has to make some effort to hide a bit, or the birds will flare—usually not enough to pass you by totally, but enough to give you a tougher shot than you'd otherwise have.

Dove decoys are used by some people, but for the most part, these are of little consequence. There are even dove calls on the market—again, probably to lure in buyers more than doves. I'm sure some people swear by them. I'm not one of those people.

Because dove hunting often involves several people, a network of hunters will often work together locating spots to shoot and keeping tabs on the flocks of birds as they switch fields. This gang also keeps track of the harvest conditions so that they can anticipate the next area

Nick Sisley with a limit of Pennsylvania mourning doves, perhaps the most-missed bird in North America. Sisley has chosen the single sighting plane of an over/under for this against-the-sky shooting. Photo by Nick Sisley.

doves will be using. And a fair number of shooters is needed to keep the birds stirred up in productive fields.

Alas, the chance to get your carcass sprinkled with fine shot is the greatest in the dove fields. The shot may not have much punch left to it, but since it rains down on folks who are looking up, the chance for eye injury is heightened. If you never wear shooting glasses anywhere else, wear them in the dove fields—please.

Although a good dove gun is one you can hit doves with, probably a gun equipped with screw-in chokes is the best. Some days the birds come right in on you, and other days they don't; with a pocketful of chokes, you can adjust quickly. The dove gun can also have some pretty good weight behind it, because you won't be swinging it that quickly—you'll probably use a variation of the sustained lead most of the time, or the swing-through method. You won't be carrying it that much, either, and you may end up shooting a lot of shells, so something a little heavier that soaks up recoil helps.

I like a gas-operated auto-loader for dove hunting, and make mine a 20. One ounce of either #8 or #7½ shot is about right through a choke that patterns a tight improved cylinder, and on most days the

Doves aren't really fearful of humans, but these shooters should make more of an attempt to stay hidden, because the birds, upon seeing them, will drift away, making for longer shots.

misses are my fault, not the gun's—no matter what you hear me scream.

The auto-loader absorbs the recoil of the load better than any fixed-breech shotgun such as a double or pump, and the long, heavy forend puts weight out at the end of the swing where it will do some good. Since dove hunting is almost always a warm-weather sport, you're rarely bundled up in heavy clothing, which has a tendency to soften recoil; so the gas mechanism's recoil-softening is even more apparent.

White wing doves, found in the American Southwest and in great numbers into Mexico, are close relatives of the mourning dove, and most of what we know about mourners applies to white wings. However, the white wing seems in most cases to be a higher bird, requiring a bit more choke; an open modified in 20-gauge or any gun that handles an ounce of shot well will do a good job on white wings.

Last year in Mexico, some Texas cronies and I shot at a lot of white wings. Mexico is a mecca for this type of shooting, and the liberal limits border on immoral. I kept my shooting within reason, even by American standards, preferring to practice on certain shots that give me trouble.

While in Mexico, I stayed at the Hacienda de Santa Engracia in the state of Tamaulipus, located about four hours, by car, south of Mc-

Allen, right on the southern tip of Texas. The white wings come out of the mesquite in the morning and again in the afternoon into the fields to feed on sunflower seeds, Johnson grass, and maize heads. When they come over, it's a spectacle.

But flock shooting will get you nothing, so the best chance takes place when the birds are returning to cover in ones and twos. But when they come out in the morning and afternoon, brother, it's like the best English driven shoot you can imagine; and with a tail wind, the birds are almost impossible to hit—you can't make yourself lead them far enough to connect. One bird with four shells is good; one with five is average or slightly above.

Where the mourning dove dips and slides, the white wing uses brute speed, with a lot of mobility, to get past you. It cuts and veers, but not with the twitching motion of the mourning dove, which seems to dive and swing even when not disturbed.

By the way, if you want to go to Mexico for a shoot of any kind, do yourself a favor: Let an outfitter handle the paperwork. Don't try doing all that stuff yourself. I used Randy Hoyt at The Detail Com-

The white wing dove of Mexico and the American Southwest is as fast as a mourning dove— maybe faster—but doesn't seem to have the erratic moves of the mourning dove. Limited seasons are held each year in the U.S., but this is mostly a tropical or subtropical species, and decent numbers require a trip south of the Rio Grande.

pany in Houston, Texas, and his outfit did a superb job of making everyone happy with the food, accommodations, shooting, and camaraderie.

Some lads regularly jump shoot doves, walking them up in their feeding areas. I've not done this much, but when I have, the doves have usually won. They seem to jump a long range, their first flurry is almost straight up, and I usually end up shooting under, behind, or both. Since walk-up dove shooting does not lend itself well to dog work, I don't do it much, preferring to do my missing where I can stand in the shade instead of walking in the sun.

Many times, trees surrounding a dove field are hotspots because doves will often land in them to look things over before flying in to feed. The shots, then, are quite easy at targets that are almost stationary. Some of the long strings of hits you hear about on doves are made this way or around watering areas; very few long runs are made on doves flighting in hard to feed in the afternoon.

As far as shot size goes, a good combination is a fairly open barrel and an ounce of #8 shot, backed by a second, tighter barrel using #7½ – this in a double. In a repeating gun, the first shell can be a #8 followed by subsequent loads of 7½s. But many times the shooting is at incoming doves where the first shot is likely to be the longest and the follow-up shots at birds that have flown in closer. Then reverse the order and put the 7½ first, followed by the 8s.

Dove hunting, taking place during hot weather as it does so often, lends itself to some little niceties that the other upland sports don't. For example, a cooler carrying chilled drinks is nice to have around – no alcohol, please – and a stool to sit on is a lot more comfortable than a fire ant hill or a rock. There isn't really a need for camo clothing, but most of the good shooters wear it because the birds flare less. Drab colors, though, should be the norm for dove hunting anywhere.

A handguard on a double does a couple of things. First, it keeps your hand off barrels hot from shooting and from insufficient heat dispersal because of the normally warm temperatures. Also, the handguard places your leading hand farther out on the barrels, which makes for a smoother swing – something dove hunters could use more of.

Many of the best dove shots don't mount the gun until they are ready to go after the bird, then they do so aggressively with the swing-through method. But most probably use the sustained lead method, precise and effective, provided they don't get lazy and slow things down. It's almost impossible to miss a speeding dove by shooting too far ahead; for every one missed that way, a million are missed behind.

A fast load helps some. That's why the 28-gauge is popular among dove hunters who know the area they hunt will offer shots inside thirty yards. The 28-gauge's extra bit of speed can make the difference between a hit up front and a charge of shot passing harmlessly through the tail feathers.

2

Woodcock

The woodcock, it is said, was put together from spare parts pulled from the near-empty bins left after the rest of the birds were made. Lots of people say this. Shows what *they* know.

The woodcock tastes a little funny, they say. Shows what *they* know. But if *you* don't like the taste of woodcock, you're better off spending your time hunting grouse or some other white-meated bird.

The American woodcock is a strange bird among today's upland game birds. But not for those reasons, because they're wrong—although I'm sure I'll get an argument about the taste. The fact is, he's strange for a few reasons not thought of very often.

First, unlike a pheasant or a grouse or a few others, he doesn't run ahead of your dog and flush wild out of range. Gentlemanly behavior is strange, these days. But he *will* run ahead and flush out of sight, so he's not a complete aristocrat.

Second, he can almost always be counted on to give you good

sport when he's around, presenting challenging shots in fine cover at a beautiful time of year. No tromping for miles through fruitless, empty acres to find him, not if you know where to look. You just park your car, load your gun, and knock on his door to say hello. Well, *almost* that easy.

The woodcock is the traditionalist's bird. With the possible exception of the bobwhite quail in the plantation country of the Deep South, there is no bird around whose devotees spend more time worrying if things are just right—not even grouse hunters.

The woodcock is a rarity because, like only the dove, he is a migrator among upland birds, and his comings and goings have long been a mystery; they still are to a certain extent. The flights come in the night and they're gone on the wind, and for a few days or possibly a week, they offer the greatest shooting at the greatest time of year.

Like the grouse hunter—who is the one most likely to divide his time between grouse and woodcock—the woodcock man leans toward English setters and double guns and tweed hats with the brims snapped down. The woodcock is a gentleman, and he is hunted by those who admire this in him and try to cultivate it in themselves.

Woodcock, whose behavior is sometimes considered strange, elicit some rather bizarre things from those who call themselves woodcock hunters. I once saw Galen Winter, a lawyer friend of mine, on three consecutive flushes, fumble with the safety on his double (miss), fumble with the rear trigger (two misses), and then forget to load his gun (I gave him credit for two misses, but he's under appeal). I know another shooter who left a high-paying job, moved eighteen hundred miles, and took a thirty percent pay cut so that he could live and work in woodcock country. I know a group of loonies who spend four days every autumn camping out in the rain and eating each other's bad cooking so that they can hunt woodcock.

I've even heard of a case where a man is reputed to know of another man who once heard of a guy who was an acquaintance of a fellow who is said to have once had a dog that would retrieve woodcock, but I've always sort of doubted that one.

In my neck of the woods, some of us put everything else on hold while the woodcock are coming through, and when I say "everything," I mean daughters' weddings, jobs, anniversaries, and appendectomies.

Woodcock, as you probably know, are relatives of the shore birds. And, for some unknown reason, they left the shore and moved into the uplands years ago. But instead of being misplaced, they are beautifully adapted for the life they have chosen, or have had thrust upon them. Rather than being made up of spare parts, they are perfect examples of self-imposed genetic engineering: evolution.

First, their being migratory in nature should tell you something about what they eat—it isn't there all year, so when the food supply vanishes, the birds leave. This food supply is mostly—almost totally—invertebrate animal matter: fish worms, fellas. They find these little creatures when they are the most active, at night, by probing the rich soils of the damp lowlands with specially built prehensile bills. These bills can be jammed into the mud right up to the hilt—the bird's face—and still the end of the bill can open to grasp a nightcrawler. And, since the food supply is most active at night (when do you catch your nightcrawlers for fishing, and why do they call them nightcrawlers?), the bird is adapted for night movement—actually, movement just after sunset and just before dawn. A bird of the twilight, he is large-eyed to see better in low-light conditions and always seems especially peppy on cloudy, overcast days.

The migratory behavior has also endowed the bird with a large breast that's well supplied with blood, making for dark meat. Since he walks little, being a bit ungainly for that function, his legs and thighs have remained white meat—just the opposite of grouse, pheasant, and quail. His heart, like those of the other migrating birds, is large for his size.

The woodcock's ears are located at the base of his bill for better sensing of the movement of worms beneath the surface—the better to hear you with, my dear—while those large eyes are set high and back on the head so he can probe the soil and still keep track of what's going on around him.

His large feet—large right from birth, really—buoy him up over spongy surfaces. The female, who migrates north as eggs are developing, is larger than the male. Their color is a rich, muted display of autumn.

The woodcock's brain has been twisted by the force of evolution so that the cerebellum—the part that controls the voluntary muscles—is up top (it's at the skull's base in humans) where it can grow, giving the bird excellent control of his motor muscles, especially his wings. You don't see a 'cock busting through branches like the grouse; instead, he flits his way around them because his navigational system for this is superior to that of any other brush-dwelling bird.

The woodcock is a great nester. The female lays four eggs, and perhaps three of the potential chicks will be born to scurry about; and the woodcock does not have near the number of natural predators that grouse do. The chicks, because they are born with a fairly long

A sure sign of woodcock: the tracks and the boring holes in moist ground. A 28-gauge shell has been placed here to show the relative size of these markings.

bill, that grows almost as you watch, split the shell from pole to pole at birth rather than along the equator like other birds.

The woodcock does best in the brushlands and the returning forests. Like the ruffed grouse, he seeks out the new, emerging forests that follow disturbances by fire, wind, and clearcutting. Also like the ruffed grouse, he is one of the first creatures to begin inhabiting farmland after it starts returning to early forest stages. In fact, if anything, the woodcock takes to such cover before the grouse. Where a clearcut may be five or six years old in some cases before grouse take an interest, woodcock will often move in after only two or three years.

In the Great Lakes states where clearcutting of aspen has helped so many species of wildlife, woodcock move in quickly, often using the bare areas where the logging equipment once sat as singing grounds in the spring. Their aerial courtship display is a fascinating aspect of the birds' behavior, although I won't go into too much detail here, other than to say that open areas near young forest are great spots to sit and watch at twilight as a male woodcock carries on his "sky dance" to attract females. For the bird hunter, keeping track of his little friends in ways other than down a shotgun's rib gives an added

An even surer sign: whitewash on the leaf of a bigtooth aspen. Woodcock droppings rarely stay around long; sometimes even a heavy dew will wash them away. So when you see droppings as fresh as this, be ready, because the woodcock is almost always close by.

dimension to his sport, and the woodcock is a prime candidate for some off-season observation.

Besides the courtship display, woodcock banding attracts followers in the spring. After nesting and hatching the young, the female woodcock and her offspring are ripe for banding. As with banded waterfowl, much is learned from the information returned off these bands, whether they come from birds that have been shot or are picked up by banders who catch the same bird again at a later time. It's possible to learn a lot about nesting habits and—especially—movements of the birds.

In banding, the most important aid is your bird dog, preferably a steady one who doesn't do something like leap in and start eating baby woodcock. A brood is first located by the dog's point. Then, Rover is tied to a handy tree, and all hands start scouring the brush for the tiny birds—scouring with the eyes and not the feet, because you can tromp on a bird easily. Once located, the birds can be easily picked up at this age and banded on their legs (one band per bird). Data is recorded, like time, place, and the bird's age (determined by the length of the bill, which grows at a steady rate from birth). The mother woodcock is usually captured by a net tossed over her, although she'll often flush before you can do it.

Banding is a great sport in itself at a great time of year, and it helps out a lot of great people.

Woodcock like aspen, but not for the buds, as do grouse. Rather, they seek the trees' thick growth. Woodcock like high stem densities, and they'd sit down in a field of metal fence posts if the posts were close enough together. So, wherever there are high concentrations of young trees, you're likely to find woodcock.

Alder is a good source for finding woodcock, although it has to be young alder, not too old or thinned out. Alder is a nitrogen-fixing plant, one that can put nitrogen directly into the soil, thus it makes its own fertility. This fertility attracts worms, which attract the woodcock. And alder is a plant of the lowlands where the moisture also attracts the food of woodcock.

Pastures are great feeding areas, especially active ones—there's nothing like a bunch of meadow muffins to enrich the soil and draw the worms that draw the birds.

Woodcock feeding cover is very often separate from woodcock resting cover that the birds use to while away the daylight hours. But they will feed in the resting cover at any time of the day if there's food available, especially when the migration is on. A few times at or near midday, I've shot woodcock that still had wriggling nightcrawlers in their bills.

In much of the United States, alder is *the* cover for woodcock, and you have a chance to actually separate grouse cover from woodcock cover when you make your hunting choices. But where grouse and woodcock are both at their highest concentrations—in the lake states of Minnesota, Wisconsin, and Michigan—the two birds are found interspersed in the same types of young forest, the woodcock being found even on the drier uplands during the day.

Often the resting cover can be identified and located by watching birds flight in at twilight to a feeding area. There is a certain pasture I know of that sits low in a hollow. The gentle cows that inhabit that land look at visiting woodcock hunters as friends and often moo a greeting. One evening, more years ago than I care to remember, I leaned against their fence and watched as woodcock after woodcock swung in over the trees, landed in the pasture, and started to feed. In all, there must have been forty birds there before the sun dropped and I couldn't see them anymore.

The next night I was back, but this time to do more than observe. I had in my hand a 7½-minute quadrangle map issued by the United

The perfect coloration of a woodcock makes him nearly invisible to an onlooker. The bird has such confidence in this camouflage that he holds as the setter slides into a point (background).

States Geologic Survey. This topo map gave me a good idea of what the land was like in every direction around the pasture. I again watched the birds arrive when the sun's candlepower was just so. Using the map and a compass, I backtracked the birds—sort of the reverse of lining a bee tree—and found on the map a small, twenty-acre bench among the hills. The next day, my dog and I set off according to the compass coordinates I'd guessed at the night before. We got lost for a little while, for we were in wild country, but finally found the bench. It was a hill whose knob had burned some years before and had come back in young aspen, and there the woodcock were spending the daylight hours, waiting for the sun to fade so they could fly the two thousand yards to the pasture to feed. There we got our limit, my dog and I.

In areas where clearcutting has taken place and alder is part of the forest makeup, you can find woodcock almost like clockwork—sometimes. In Wisconsin, there is a public hunting area that was cut over

By far the best resting cover for woodcock consists of young stands of second-growth aspen. Those that have been managed as part of game department policy or are commercially managed for pulpwood production are the best. When the stands also hold small clumps of young speckled alder, so much the better.

some years back. While hunting this cut, my partner and I found that the aspen itself held few birds, but each clump of alder interspersed in the wet areas within the cut held a bird or two. Great shooting.

But it is the flights that woodcock hunters live for, those almost magical arrivals of birds fresh from the north. Woodcock migrate as individuals, so the new arrivals may number one to scores, with each bird making his own choice for himself; the flock rule does not apply as it does to waterfowl.

Woodcock will follow stream and river valleys in a southerly direction, waiting for winds from a northern quadrant to push them along their desired route. A south wind holds them where they are, for these small birds do not wish to fight a head wind. The river valleys provide the food they need and probably also serve as navigational aids; the valley winds usher them south. If you have a pet cover in a valley that runs north–south, check it the morning after a north wind when the flights are in progress—you'll likely find birds.

Woodcock, depending upon kindly Nature for migrational assistance, go quite early—as early as mid-October in their northern range,

How to approach a pointed woodcock? In this picture, the dog has made a find on the edge of a piece of good-looking cover. The hunter approaches with gun at the ready in case the bird flushes early . . .

. . . and then circles so that he is coming in on the dog. The bird is trapped between dog and shooter and has only one real option: straight up, which in this cover is among the easiest of all woodcock shots.

correspondingly later in the south. Thus, if you await the hard freezes to hunt these birds' migration, you'll be too late. The females—the proven breeders—go first. Chunkier, they migrate early to take advantage of the better weather and better food supply as a safeguard against bad winds that can stall them. The smaller males stay north longer, perhaps to imprint their singing grounds better. When your bag contains mostly or all male birds, you are close to the end of the flights and the 'cock season, no matter what the game regulations tell you.

The shooting of a woodcock is dependent upon many things, the first being your dog. Simply, a pointing dog is the best and the most fun for woodcock. These birds were made for a setter, Brittany, pointer, or any of the breeds that stand their birds. Even though very old tradition dictates a cocker spaniel—which is where the "cocker" part of his name comes from, as in "woodcocker"—our more recent tradition names a pointing breed.

Yes, contrary to what you've heard, woodcock do run from under a point. I've disagreed with those people who say it never happens; yet it does, but only early in the season, when the native birds are around. (I think that flight birds, encountered a moment or two after their arrival, are too pooped to ambulate.) But the birds don't run far, and they don't run fast; even an average dog can make some great finds and points on woodcock. Woodcock make a dog look good—period.

When flushed, a woodcock, especially the female, will often head for openings in the canopy of leaves. The males seem to bore out low and faster—well they *are* faster. If you approach the pointing dog with this in mind, you can often set yourself up with some straightaway shots.

But the woodcock jumps vertically most times, and this dictates a high-shooting gun. And the woodcock's fragile nature takes away the need for coarse shot driven by ear-splitting powder charges. I suppose that if you hold off on any marginal shots, you could even use a .410, but I'm set against this bore for any bird. With woodcock, there's always a chance of moving a grouse, and the .410 user is going to shoot what he has with him—the .410—and that's asking for trouble.

Among many, lately, the swift-moving little 28-gauge is a favorite woodcock piece. This gauge's load moves quickly, blessed with a bore diameter/shot column length that harmonize with each other to produce a hard-hitting, short shot string. And the gun itself is normally made to a lighter weight. It's sweet, especially with three-quarter-ounce skeet loads (#9 shot).

But, if you are going to shoot woodcock, the 20 is the choice of thousands, so consider: This gauge is normally light, has efficient ballistics, and a good choice of loads. The standard seven-eighths-to-one-ounce 20-gauge loads are fine for woodcock, but pick a small size—#9 is deadly from an open barrel; the market hunters used 10s. For close-in, fifteen-foot shots, you can go to #7½, seven-eighth ounce. You won't ruin any birds and won't have to pass up too many ultra-close chances.

For all that is said of woodcock guns, few people venture beyond the 20-gauge. I have, and I like it—my 16-gauge grouse gun being also my 16-gauge woodcock gun, because the birds hold in the same coverts for most of the year where I hunt. It's especially effective after leaf fall progresses and shots are longer. This gun weighs like a 20 and handles fast. I shoot one-ounce powder-puff loads of #8 shot and, like the 28, this combination seems to kill better than it should. In most years, I start off with a 28 and then switch to a 16 after the leaves drop and cover thins.

Some hunters venture into the land of the 12-gauge when hunting woodcock. These folks are normally users of an expensive British or continental game gun in that bore. But the guns themselves are usually around six pounds, and you can go with a light one-ounce load or even a lighter hand-loaded shell. The gun weight gets critical only if you are carrying too much weight for a certain gauge. In my opinion, a man shooting a six-and-one-half-pound 20 is not helping himself if he leaves his six-pound 12 at home. He can load his lighter 12 like a 20 and get better patterns out of it.

Remember that big cerebellum I mentioned earlier? Well, it allows the woodcock to cut some fancy skid marks in the air, usually about the time you're ready to shoot. And, since woodcock flush close, the chances of evasive flying increase. This combination means a muzzle-light balancing, allowing instant movement by the forend hand to adjust to the flight of the bird. A gun that balances rear of the hinge pin—about three inches ahead of the trigger (front trigger on a double-trigger gun)—feels and handles fast. It also feels lighter for the same weight gun as a piece of different balance, because the weight is in your "strong" hand close to your body, and you have less lifting and moving of that weight during the mount and swing.

In most woodcock cover, especially in the early season, "swing" is a cruel joke. Most shots are snap shots taken now or not at all. With pheasants, you shoot for the head; with woodcock, you shoot at the part of the bird you can see, and poke and stab are the shooting rules.

This gentlemanly bird lends himself to some gentlemanly forms of hunting. I like sort of strolling through woodcock cover—around it if I can—while my dog is inside checking on the opposition. When her bell stops, I can usually fight my way in and get the shot.

Walking logging trails that are still passable through cutover areas while the dog works the edges is also grand sport. I've got a friend who does his woodcocking with a superbly trained English pointer. He follows along with his over/under 20 carried on a shoulder sling. He sums it up: "I'm taking a walk in the woods; when the dog points, that's when I start hunting."

Some days the birds prefer some rather unlikely cover. I've shot woodcock in small clumps of trees in the middle of acres of Christmas trees, and sumac-covered hillsides near low feeding cover should never be passed up. The overhead protection from the sumac offers the birds what they want—cover. They'll feed in the lowlands and then fly into the cover afterward.

Woodcock hunters, if they're successful, should have a regular string of coverts and shouldn't overshoot any one. You'd better guard

them, too, because someone will take your coverts if you're too generous, coming back alone when you're not around. I've had it done to
me, and I've done it to others—it's the American way.

In England, where the woodcock's larger cousin is shot, the bird is
considered a real find. On a drive for pheasants, the only time the
drivers (beaters) are allowed to talk is when they flush a woodcock
that's heading out and over the "guns." Then, a crisp "Cock up!" can
be heard.

Curiously, shooting doubles on woodcock is tough. I've shot a
very large number of these birds, and I've never had a double—
haven't had even a chance. Well, once, but I had my limit and my gun
was empty. But you read and hear a lot about doubles on woodcock.
I've had doubles and even triples on a number of game birds because
the rest will present you with the chance, but not 'cock—not very
often.

In wingshooting, a true double is a simultaneous rise of two birds,
or two birds in the air before you start shooting. If a bird flushes and
you shoot it, then you collect another that flushes, you've not shot a
double but two closely spaced singles. I think most doubles on woodcock are of this type. In England, a double ("right and left") will
usually get you something dandy from the organizer of the hunt as a
remembrance—like a good bottle of warming liquid.

One mistake shooters of doubles (the gun, not the feat) make that
gets them in trouble is shooting a bird and then immediately breaking
the gun to reload. At about that moment, a couple times a year,
another bird will take off and you'll be standing there with a broken
gun. A young friend from Texas joined me a couple of years ago for a
shoot in Michigan, and I warned him of this a couple of times the first
day. On the second day, it happened to him—but not since. You've got
to learn from your own mistakes.

In the eastern part of the United States, the woodcock population
has been down over the past few years, resulting in shortened seasons and lowered bag limits, while in the western part of the bird's
range, everything's doing fine. There are a number of explanations for
this, among them the shooting of the birds on their wintering grounds
by sportsmen in the South. I don't buy that one, because I know of
very few southern woodcock hunters, and I get down that way quite
often. Sounds like the normal "blame-it-on-them-guys" excuse that
northern game managers are so adept at; many of them make entire
careers out of making excuses and retire with gold watches and par-
ties and pensions and the whole deal.

I think the problem is loss of habitat, the new growth that is not coming up because of the lack of cutting and proper wildlife management. Most of the best vegetation in New England—vegetation that came in forty to fifty years ago as the Depression gobbled up farms and converted them to deeds on a bank-vault shelf—is no longer down low like it was when the farms reverted from pasture to woods. Instead, that vegetation is now sixty feet in the air at the wrong end of a mature maple tree. It is often fruitless trying to convince a state that you can't have woodcock *and* beautiful climax forests that make picture postcard sights in autumn.

I had a guest in from Massachusetts for a shoot some years back. The first day, we pulled up near a great cover, and as we loaded our guns, he looked at the brush, dropped his mouth open, and asked something like: "Are we going in *there*?" Seems the cover he hunted at home was a lot more open because it was mature or maturing. At home, a good day saw him move five woodcock. We flushed, as I remember, forty-four in half a day. We did it "in *there*."

3

Ruffed Grouse

Now, first off, let me tell you that when it comes to ruffed grouse, I'm biased as hell. They may well be one of the two best game birds on this continent—the other being the woodcock, a most happy fella who often shares the same coverts with "The King."

Doves test our marksmanship, pheasants our tenacity, and Huns our legs, but the ruffed grouse tests all of these—and more. First, let's see why he's king, let's see how history has treated him and how he's treated us, and let's see what it is that sets him so far above other some say lesser—birds.

Throughout the course of American sporting literature, volumes have been dedicated to this bird. Such classics as *New England Grouse Shooting*, the *Tranquillity* series, *Grouse of the North Shore*, *My Friend the Partridge*, and others have been devoted all or in part to this bird. Part of the reason for this attention is historical and sociological in nature: The first outdoor writers were from New England, and it is there that this gamebird held—and holds—sway. Naturally, the boys wrote about their favorite.

Part of the reason for the lure of grouse and grouse hunting is the civilized nature of the bird. He does not migrate—he's there all year to watch, to listen to as he drums in the spring, and maybe to enjoy as the broods grow and develop and scare the devil out of you as you wander along a trout spring in the late summer. He seems, of all things, a gentlemanly bird, and he seems to inspire a gentlemanly set of codes among those who pursue him. I wish I had a nickel of every dollar that was spent only in the last ten years for boots and hats and vests and other items just for grouse hunting. I wouldn't even need a cut of the money spent on guns and vehicles and on trips here and there.

Part of the reason for the lure of grouse and grouse hunting is the wild, untamed nature of the bird. Here is an animal that cannot be reared in captivity without its losing the wildness. Here is a bird that haunts the upland wilderness, yet takes quite nicely to the clearcuts and managed areas created for him and him alone. Here is a bird that flushes with such abandon that he has, variously, impaled himself on limbs, poked eyes out on twigs, broken wings that are near the breaking point from the stress of the flush, and scared hell out of generations of would-be grouse shooters. Here is a bird that makes us feel like beginners every time we have to shoot at him, and one whose daily limit could easily be a case of fun and games by the game department people. I can hear them now in the state capital: "Hey, guys, let's drive 'em nuts and tell 'em the limit is five a day. Bet they'll strip their gears trying to get five in a *season!*" (I know sarcasm when I read it.)

Part of the reason why grouse are so popular is that they reflect, almost, the unattainable. Nobody is always a consistently good grouse shot. Oh, you'll have your days just as I've had mine, but they don't come often, brother, and they ain't easily forgotten. On that vast majority of days that we can call "others," we're just as likely to miss everything. And the funny thing is, it doesn't really matter. If we miss five grouse in a day and never cut a feather, we come away glad that there are at least five grouse left for us to chase the next day or week.

Part of the reason why grouse are so difficult to bag is their habitat. These are birds of the thick, young forests that have only recently grown back. Where once it was pastureland, for example, this land went through the seral stages of grasses, shrubs, and finally into the young growth of trees that the grouse need. As we'll see, they need trees in various age classes, and sometimes these age classes are best created by clearcutting entire areas of all trees—the twentieth century's socially acceptable form of clearing that does the very thing storms and fire did before white man arrived here: create openings in the forest canopy where the young trees can grow.

Sadly, much of the country has "gone past" for good grouse country, especially in the storied New England shooting grounds. Where once the Great Depression reduced hardscrabble farms from fields and pastures to young woodlands—and grouse cover—now those young forests have matured and are the homes of squirrels and turkeys and other species that need a mature forest.

This thick growth places a premium on the shooting skill of grouse hunters. The grouse is a bird of explosive flush and flight, getting up to speed before he comes into sight and hurtling through the cover so that some days you feel that even an accurately pointed charge will never catch up with him. The shooting defies the swing theory of wingshooting, which simply says that you have to swing ahead of the bird and fire. No, most grouse shooting is a snap-shooting proposition, one of aim-and-you'll-miss. Instead, the practiced brush shooter points his gun ahead of the bird right from the git-go, stays there, and triggers his shot when the butt touches his shoulder. Grouse hunters are among the fastest shots in the world, and among the best. Most shoot doubles, either side-by-sides or over/unders, because these handle faster, and you need all the help you can get.

Hunting grouse is not especially difficult in terms of tactics. It doesn't take the scouting and backcountry research that dove hunting does, and it doesn't require the devotion to planning and tactics that pheasant hunting needs. Instead, grouse hunting takes being able to identify grouse cover—practice so that you can do it while on the interstate. After a while, a piece will just "feel" grousy.

Grouse live across much of North America, one time even thriving as far south as Arkansas. But they do best where aspen trees are in the forest. Specifically, where aspen dominate. Grouse use young—very young—aspens for brood cover. Here the chicks are safe from the prying eyes and the talons of birds of prey such as goshawks and great horned owls. The term "goshawk" is actually a bastardization of "grouse hawk," and aspen stands with trees only inches apart—tiny trees not much bigger than your thumb—defeat these birds. Such stands also have high insect concentrations. Grouse chicks need to eat bugs right after hatching for tissue development.

Grouse also use slightly older, more thinned-out stands of aspen as drumming cover. Here the males will establish their territories and will drum as a way of validating their claims and also as a means of attracting females, which then trundle off to nest near the base of a large tree. These birds also use large aspen—trees over twenty years old—as a source of food in the winter, feeding on the buds of the aspens. These buds are loaded with nutrition, and thus the birds are able to get what they need with a minimum amount of time investment, making them less likely to be picked off by predators. Where aspen are not present, the birds must eat more of the available lower-quality foods, and they then suffer higher losses to predation because they're out in the open longer.

Unlike pheasant and quail, ruffed grouse are actually aided by deep snow cover during the winter. As snow-roosting birds, grouse will tunnel their way under fluffy snow and—igloo-style—stay relatively warm when the outside temperatures nudge twenty below zero or worse. In the Great Lakes states, where grouse enjoy their highest numbers because of the aspen ecosystem, a winter of deep snow is often followed by a good grouse season because of the high rate of survival.

Actually, ruffed grouse experience their highest rate of mortality during the fall, when broods are breaking up and the young birds are scattering to stake out their own territories. This "fall shuffle" disperses the broods to fill available habitat, but not without a price. During the fall shuffle, one percent per day of the total population can be lost for a period of several weeks, until the young birds have either found a safe place or gotten picked off by one of the various forms of death that await reckless young grouse.

You've probably heard of and seen grouse doing things like flying into the sides of houses, smashing into telephone wires, flying into trees, and so forth. This "crazy season," as it used to be called, takes a number of the young birds out of the picture, birds that would otherwise have had a pretty good chance at survival. Many states start their hunting seasons to take advantage of high populations—before brood breakup gets underway too heavily. This way, grouse are shot that would die anyway.

In Michigan, for example, the grouse season starts September 15 each year. In many cases, the broods are still intact at this time—but they aren't easy to hit. The hunting activity further scatters the broods. Before the season was moved back to September 15, the traditional Michigan opener was October 1, but many people in the Michigan Department of Natural Resources rightly felt that the extra two weeks' wait took a lot of potential grouse out of hunters' bags through natural attrition from the fall shuffle.

However, the pheasant-quail psychology holds in some circles.

Grouse that survive the autumn shuffle and the high predation rates (don't forget, baby hawks and owls born in the spring are on their own in the fall, too—and hungry) and have made it safely, through sheer luck, to adequate cover should be left alone. Since grouse have less of a problem with winter than do pheasants and quail, which don't snow burrow, they should not be hunted after December 1. At that point, hunting becomes an *additive* mortality factor, not *compensatory*. In other words, autumn hunting takes birds that would die anyway through natural causes (compensatory); winter hunting takes birds that would otherwise have had a good chance of surviving (additive).

In the fall, the grouse is at his best. The cover helps him; you can push him out of one patch of aspen and he'll find another. He's full of P and V, daring you and your dog to find him and stop him. In the winter, moving a grouse may mean moving it out of the only cover still standing after the cold and snow have worked it over, thus making him a tired, cold, exposed, and confused potential victim of a hawk, owl, or fox. In the winter the leaves are down and good shooters can run up some pretty impressive strings of hits. Tacky.

One of the problems that grouse hunters have to contend with is the very real existence of the grouse's population cycle. Running about seven years from high to high (or low to low), this cycle results in populations that can be either very good or horrible.

In good years across the lake states, thirty flushes a day can be had by a man and a dog working good cover all day. In poor years in poor cover, one or two flushes a day is about the norm. Grouse come in a variety of color phases, but the predominant two are the grey birds and the brown birds. In years of high populations, the brown birds are quite numerous; in bad years, you're likely to move only the grey grouse. The grey birds are the most common in the northern part of the bird's range, perhaps because they are hardier or because their coloration is better in the winter, indicating high winter predator losses. Likewise, the effects of the cycle are more acutely felt in the northern states, probably because the brown birds come and go with the cycle but are the predominant color phase farther south. A present Wisconsin study links the grouse cycle to the hare cycle in Canada and the resulting shuffle of owls and hawks between the two.

However, happily, proper management of grouse habitat has a tendency to modify the cycle, making the lows less low while accentuating the highs. As the use of proper habitat manipulation techniques become more widespread among enlightened biologists in charge of such things, maybe the cycle won't be so bad.

The management for ruffed grouse has reached an art form. My friend Gordon Gullion of the University of Minnesota is the recognized world authority on ruffed grouse, and his studies after more than a quarter-century are very clearly focused on the manipulation of aspen for grouse habitat. That management technique requires the periodic clearcutting of aspen stands to maintain the age-class diversity grouse require. Aspen spring up like weeds after they've been clearcut, and the young growth serves first as brood cover, then – after a few years – as drumming and winter cover, and finally as winter feeding cover. After that, the old stand is clearcut and the process starts over again.

This cutting is of value not only to grouse, but to woodcock, deer, rabbits, and a myriad of non-hunted species of little birdies and beasties. It's a neat deal for everybody, even industry, because the aspen is used for paper making. Everybody wins.

With all of this as background, then, what about grouse-hunting tactics? The main tactic is to find good grouse cover – with luck, a clearcut – and make tracks through it with a good dog. Tradition dictates a pointing dog, but there are not that many really good grouse dogs. The birds will run, and they don't always hold the way we'd like them to. And when they do come off the ground, they are a tough out. Like a good football running back, they get their top speed all at once, and they make a hell of a commotion doing it. None of this, as you know, makes for good shooting averages.

During wet years – years when the summers have been fairly damp and the vegetation lush – grouse are normally scattered. In dry years, the birds are concentrated near water. Grouse don't drink, biologists say, but they need the thick cover that is found near water during dry summers, and they're normally still there when the fall season opens, regardless of recent rains. Streams, the shores of lakes and ponds – all of these are good spots in the dry years.

Looking for stands of aspen or some other low growth is a good way of finding grouse, especially if the trees are within a foot of each other and no bigger around than your wrist. This is good autumn cover, and the grouse have gravitated there during the fall shuffle. Grouse are birds of the edge, where the sun can penetrate the forest canopy and start new growth. This edge can be artificially induced, as with clearcutting, or it may be a naturally occurring phenomenon, such as the rejuvenation after a fire or windstorm. Old farm fields coming back often make for good cover. In New England, where some folks seem more devoted to big trees than to grouse, this is about the only grouse cover available, game departments being a little hesitant

Checking out good-looking grouse cover of young aspen, the best. Like good woodcock cover, it must be young, although woodcock will use young growths of trees a year or two before grouse move in. Grouse also need older aspen trees at certain times of the year. This is good fall cover; thicker is better when the young are being raised, and in the winter the birds need aspen twenty-five years or older for the buds they produce, the best food a grouse can get in the winter.

to do any clearcutting. Clearcutting makes the area look like Ground Zero right after somebody pushed the button, but in a couple of years it's lush and beautiful. The problem is, nobody gives this technique a chance.

Working into the wind helps your dog, but it isn't as imperative with grouse as it is in pheasant hunting. Still, the dog needs every advantage. Once the dog pins one for you, approach the point from the side so that the dog can see you and also so that the bird has one less option about which way to fly. Grouse will normally fly toward the thickest cover, much like quail, so positioning yourself with that in mind can give you some of the easier straightaway shots.

Unlike some species, grouse can be effectively hunted all day. I suppose the hunting is not quite as good during the middle of the day, but that's more a function of poorer scenting conditions for your dog than anything the birds do. A little rain, such as a light drizzle, is good if you can stand the wet cover, but a downpour is better waited out—it washes away scent and the birds are covered up, normally in conifers where you can't get a shot anyway.

Windy days make the birds skittish, clean the cover of scent very quickly, and are better spent in a duck blind. I've never done well in the wind; I can't hear the birds get up, and my dog loses the scent easily. Still, I'd rather hunt in the wind than not hunt at all.

Most grouse shooting is a snap-shot proposition. There's rarely time to go through the whole drill and establish lead consciously. Instead, the best grouse shots use well-fitting guns that handle quickly; and they don't dwell on the target. In fact, if you ask someone about a successful shot he just made on grouse, he's likely to tell you that he doesn't know where he was pointing when the gun went off, other than he knows he wasn't behind. The grouse in hand tells you he was right.

The best, most pleasant and effective gun to shoot for upland birds is one that has its weight centered between the hands. The exception to this is the gun the experienced grouse—and woodcock—hunter carries. Here a distinct barrel lightness helps, the weight being centered rear of the hinge pin on a double—or somewhere about three inches ahead of the trigger.

My old standby grouse and woodcock gun is a Parker 16-gauge, bored open improved cylinder and a light modified. The gun weighs just shy of six pounds, and that weight is carried toward the rear. The barrels and forearm of this gun weigh exactly what the barrels and forearm of my 20-gauge quail gun weigh, so you can see that the weight isn't out front.

Such a gun is hard to master—I'll let you know how I did it once I do—but it is the premier brush-shooting weapon for these birds. That's why you'll rarely see an experienced grouse hunter switching guns for this bird: Once he finds something that works, he stays with it.

Happily, this is one of the shooting sports that folks seem to get better at with the passing years. An example is a good friend of mine, a fine gentleman named Al Smith (no relation, but I, at least, wish he were), who is a former national president of the Ruffed Grouse Society. He is the first living person to have had a chapter of the organization named for him. Al is past seventy, but he's fit, and he lives for grouse hunting, his law practice taking second place all autumn.

Al shoots a little custom-made 28-gauge at grouse and woodcock, and he does very well—as well as he did thirty years ago, he says. I believe it, because most days he outshoots me. By the way, if you worry that age will steal away your lightning reflexes, forget it. Reaction time is a constant throughout a person's lifetime. If you keep eyes, arms, and wrists in good shape, you can be almost as fast at eighty as at forty.

On the other hand, there are a lot of grouse alive right now that would otherwise be holding down a plate of wild rice if more people were a little slower. Often we snatch at birds, firing the first shot when the bird is only inches out of cover, and then drilling the next one right in there on top of it. Then, with an empty gun, we watch the bird sail away, in good range for what seems like forever. It's hard to wait out grouse, but it can be done, especially in the later days of autumn when the cover has thinned so that you can see more than a few yards.

Any bird fired at should be followed up. Grouse can't carry much lead, but they often give no indication that they've been hit. Every year I find a bird I thought I missed just by following it up. I don't mean push the poor devil incessantly, but try for a reflush; you may get the bird or at least satisfy yourself that the first shot was your normal miss. Any bird that suddenly twitches or changes course at your shot should be followed; often these are signs of a hit.

Barrels for grouse guns are usually short. I don't think that barrel *length* has as much to do with handling as barrel *weight*. One gun I use on occasion is a 16 with twenty-eight-inch barrels. A London-built game gun, this piece has barrels that weigh what the Parker's twenty-six-inchers weigh. I see no difference, because if I smack the gun against a tree, I usually hit some part of the gun other than the last two inches of the barrels. But, generally, twenty-five- and twenty-six-inch barrels *weigh* less than twenty-eight-inch barrels, so they're preferred. You can forget, in my opinion, about any advantage of a single sighting plane as offered by a repeater or over/under. The best grouse gun is a side-by-side double. The wide barrels are seen peripherally by the gunner as he mounts, and they are also more accurate for vertical pointing. Since most grouse and—especially—woodcock are rising when they're shot at, this is important. I always "lose" the reference point of the rib on an over/under in the brush. (I know, we don't look at barrels, but we see them nonetheless. Out of focus, but there. We just don't dwell on them. To say we don't see them *at all*—or shouldn't—insults the intelligence of anyone who's ever done much shooting.)

On the matter of gauge, the 20 is the most popular and is the widespread choice. I shoot a 16, others I know shoot light 12s. There is nothing to be gained by shooting one gauge over another if weight and balance are the same. An ounce of shot is enough, and some folks do right well with a 28-gauge. Like the 16, it's a freak because its three-quarter-ounce load just kills better than it should. The grouse doesn't have the toughness of a pheasant or even a quail, ounce for ounce, so you don't need blasting caps and nails to kill him in the air. Often a bird that's wingtipped in full flight dies crashing through the brush toward earth. A few years back, I flushed two birds out of some grey dogwood, a great feeding area, and a bird cut back over my head through some nearby aspens. I shot and was aware of the bird turning over in the air, normally a sign of a broken wing. I picked it up, still beating its wings as the gallinaceous birds are prone to do when the spinal cord is violated. When I cleaned the bird, aside from the broken wing joint, he had nary a mark on him. I think a lot of our "clean kills" are the result of a collision between a lightly hit grouse and a sturdy tree.

Gun weight, although less critical than balance, should nevertheless be manageable—a subjective judgment. For most people, a gun of five-and-a-half to six-and-a-half pounds is about right. You'll be carrying this gun a long way through some tough going, and a lot of the carrying will be with one hand as you fight off vegetation that looks like the set from *Revenge of the Plant People.* Carrying the gun with the barrels pointed up and the butt resting on the hip, a convenient position, is a good way of getting into action quickly. A gun carried this way doesn't seem to weigh as much, either.

Day in and day out, an ounce of #8 shot is probably the best, although some use a 7½ in the left barrel or as the second shot in a magazine gun.

There are those who are devoted to switching guns part of the way through the season as leaf fall and wilder birds make long shots more common than they were in the summer-lush early season. There's nothing wrong with this at all, provided that your late-season gun is decidedly like your early-season gun in weight, fit, and balance.

Actually, the only change should be one of chokes, another point in the favor of screw-in chokes in any shotgun—double or repeating gun. With the twist of a wrench, you can change the borings so that you have the fit and feel of the old familiar bird gun, but now you'll be shooting a piece that can reach out ten to fifteen yards farther. However, even in selecting a gun or chokes for late grouse hunting, you'll do well to stay on the open side of full, even as the second barrel of a double. There are just too few opportunities to justify effective forty-yard patterns compared to the times when you need a little more

A grouse dog can handle grouse—most of the time. These birds are among the most difficult there are to hunt with a pointing dog, and some dog men say it takes five hundred grouse to make a grouse dog. Author's setter, Jess, points in young aspen. A quick look at this cover will tell you why few grouse hunters use guns with long barrels; but in reality, if you hit a tree with your barrels while swinging on a grouse, it usually isn't the last two or three inches that makes contact. Sometimes it's your arm.

spread at twenty yards. The average grouse probably dies twenty-five yards from the gunner, early season or late, and the gun should reflect this fact of shooting life.

It takes a number of grouse contacts to build a good grouse dog, one that can pin and hold a bird without creeping too close to flush the bird. The timid dog, oddly enough, has a tendency to flush too many birds by bumping them. He can't make up his mind whether he should move ahead or stay put, the bird gets time to think things over, and he's gone. The bold dog—one you can control—is better because he dashes in, finds the bird, and *wham!* he's on point. The grouse, thoroughly impressed with the whole thing, sticks around to see how the end comes out and gives you the chance to miss.

Many hunters want their dogs to work close, probably fearing the dog's inability to hold a grouse. When the dog bumps the bird, the owner wants to be around for the shot. So by keeping his dog in close, the pointing-dog man is actually treating his dog as a flushing breed.

If the dog is belled so that you can tell when he's on point—because the bell stops—you should be able to let him hunt at his own speed, moving ahead in thin cover, staying closer in the good stuff. When he points, you have to go find him.

I like a grouse dog that, much like a waterfowl retriever has learned, understands and—here's the biggie—*obeys* hand signals. My own dog and I have this worked out so that only the one of us with all the feet does the tough walking. The other strolls through the woods. Jess, following my hand signals toward productive-looking cover, will let me direct her from spot to spot, while I skirt the edges. If she goes in and doesn't come out, I'll give a little whistle. If she's up to something else besides pointing, she'll move enough to tinkle her bell; if I whistle twice and I don't hear a bell, I move in. Grouse, like all upland birds, are alerted by the voice, and most grouse hunters use their voices the most often on the dog. Hand signaling keeps the talking down, and the opposition is left guessing exactly who/what/where you are.

4

Quail

Quail fall into several categories, but the bobwhite is the one who gets the most attention. Called "partridge," or just plain "bird" in the South where he is king, this bird has just about everything going for him: He is a fast target, gives a good dog a worthy opponent, and he's great on the table. No bird, with the possible exception of the woodcock, generates such affection among his followers.

Typical bobwhite hunting in years past saw sculptured dogs pointing in the broomstraw and coveys fanning out to be picked up by a good singles dog; but in much of the bird's range, this is not the case any more. Instead, the quail have taken to the thick stuff, because, frankly, that's about the only stuff there is any more.

Good quail hunting in the South is getting harder to find as private land is posted up. Much of the best hunting is now found on private hunting plantations that offer shooting in a variety of ways. Found mostly in Georgia and Florida, with some in the Carolinas, these plantations cater to out-of-state sportsmen who want to sample what once was, when places like these dotted the antebellum South.

After Reconstruction, these places were owned and operated by old-line Yankee money, and in those days, things went like this: Let's say that you were the son of a northern industrialist, a big-money family from the Northeast. Maybe you had made your money making coffee mills, like the Parker Brothers did before they turned to shotguns, or maybe you were a textile baron from New England or a timber tycoon from Michigan. Doesn't matter.

Well, long after the War Between the States (some of my readers are Southerners), the land values in the South were low. The rich folks—the ones with the vested interests to protect that helped make that war in the first place—were either dead, on the run, or had chosen not to take the Oath of Allegiance to the Union and had thus found themselves disenfranchised and landless. The carpetbaggers held sway, and many times land was illegally taken by these scalawags and sold—very often to Northerners with a taste for quailing.

So, for a few dollars an acre, maybe less, you came into possession of a large estate, let's say ten thousand acres or more. Since you didn't need the plantation to earn its keep, you turned it into a shooting man's playground.

You hired dog trainers, stablemen, field hands, house people, and an overseer—a manager. Your function, then, was to show up about the middle of November and start shooting quail. You followed the dogs—pointers—from your hunting horse, dismounting to walk in for the flush. Maybe a companion from the North joined you for a week or two. Things continued merrily until Christmas when you returned home for the holidays, coming back in January for another couple of months of shooting. Then, back North to await the next season.

As semi-absentee landlords, northern folks rankled the locals, but as quail people, they were what the doctor ordered. Many of the earliest and most complete studies on quail biology and management were paid for by these plantation owners, and these studies revealed that quail, certain crops, and timber could be managed together. The studies also revealed that periodic burning of habitat—particularly the grasses—kept the undergrowth from getting so thick that quail had a hard time in it. The basis of wildlife management, at least some of the earliest efforts, was started by these absentee quail shooters.

These are the Good Old Days you hear so much about. Never mind that two world wars were waiting on the horizon, that your teeth fell out when you were thirty-five, and that babies died of simple diseases like mumps. In those days, there were *birds*.

Today, much of that hunting is available to out-of-staters (and to in-staters, too, I guess) at a plantation devoted to quail. Such places may feature deer, turkey, or waterfowl hunting as asides, but their main focus is quail, and quail they do have. Operated as shoot-for-pay outfits, these plantations feature huge acreages—many well over twelve thousand acres—proper wildlife management, and a good population of native birds supplemented by hardy quail that are prop-agated, reared, and released by the plantation's staff. There are also bird dogs—again, pointers in the main—and dog trainers and han-dlers. Many of the top dog trials in the South are held on the grounds of some of these places.

The nicer places feature plush accommodations; dinner is a fancy affair, and the hospitality flows. If you close your eyes and imagine a little, you can see yourself as a guest of a real plantation owner, down to enjoy a shoot for a few days.

Naturally, none of this is cheap; but expense, like I tell my shoe-less kids, is relative. Usually, several hundred Yankee dollars a day, plus more for lodging and food, will take care of you in grand style. You can cut costs by driving if you're close enough, and save time by flying. You can save money or time—not normally both, and not just in quail hunting, either.

Anyway, the quail hunt goes something like this, both at these places and in the wild, where bobwhites are concerned: The non-plantation quail is likely to be in the thick stuff where he'll beat you with his speed, a covey coming up right on the edge of a swamp and all hands heading for the jungle. In there, the singles shooting is tough. The birds fly like small ruffed grouse, and they know the ropes, especially if they've been hunted a little.

Even when you catch a covey out in the open, more the norm on the big spreads, you dasn't dally. A quail, like a grouse, gets all of his speed at once. By the time you can see him emerge from thigh-high grass, he's already at top end. And twelve quail don't make twelve times as much noise and create as much confusion as one quail; they make noise like twelve quail to the twelfth power, or something expo-nential. If you look up the genealogy of the phrase "In unity there is strength," the reference book will say, "see also 'quail.'"

When a covey goes, do the best you can to select one bird. Single out one that strikes your fancy, maybe a sassy little cockbird, his white face showing clearly, or maybe you look for one on the edge of the knot of birds, or one that's going dead away from you. You'll find that a majority of your open-field shots are straightaways, that the angles

Tom Huggler draws down on a single in a Georgia field of classic cover. Such shooting is usually rare, quail being more and more birds of the brush, even in their traditional southern strongholds. Huggler favors a long left-hand hold on his short-barreled double for a smoother swing.

come in the thick cover when birds are trying to avoid you and cover at the same time.

Because of this, if you can avoid getting rattled, the shooting is not tough. That's why single-bird shooting at members of a dispersed covey is so productive—the old explosion is missing, and so is the choosing. Then, quail come easily.

If the South is the traditional stronghold of the bobwhite, the plains states of Iowa, Nebraska, and Kansas, and the border state of Missouri are the *de facto* population centers. Here—although, in contrast to the South, you're not likely to find a rubber-tired wagon pulled by matched mules—is where the real action is in this part of this century. So much of the quail country of the South is either tied up in private ownership or is no longer productive, that the vast reaches of the plains hold more birds than the South ever did; maybe not acre per acre, but certainly region for region.

If you hunt bobwhites in, say, Kansas, you'll quickly learn that they are not the same bird as Georgia quail. They come off the ground at longer ranges, and they tend to run more. Quail will run, as any gamebird will run, ahead of your dog on occasion, and in the big country of the plains, this running can put them into the air at extreme ranges. Here the shooting is a problem, because a small bird at long range indicates some pretty specialized equipment as far as your firepower is concerned.

Bobs are also hunted on many shooting preserves in this country, and there the hunter and the club manager can work out an arrange-

A male and a female bob taken from the piney woods.

ment that pretty closely approximates the traditional southern hunting; never do the shoot-for-pay places set up so that the quail gunning is like you'd find in Iowa. Hmmmmmm.

The hunting of quail usually follows a pattern that's as effective as anything you can conjure up. Quail spend the night huddled in a covey, each bird facing outward, snuggled up with his brothers and sisters for warmth and protection. Then, as danger approaches, the birds flush in a zillion different directions. Once they flush, they head for cover, and if the hapless shooter is in the way, he's just about bamboozled. The birds will just speed on by him, and he has to turn and take them going away. There's very little chance of this. Be happy they weren't lions.

So when a dog nails a covey, the smart money lines up so that the thick stuff is beyond the birds. This offers more straightaway shots than anything else.

I remember my first encounter with a covey of quail. I was in my teens, making a trip to Nebraska with my father and a friend of his. The Weimaraner we were hunting with pointed, and I walked in, expecting a rooster pheasant. Instead, the brown bombs came out of the grass, breaking from the open toward a plum thicket.

This was back in the old Soil Bank days, and the grassy fallow field we were hunting was waist high in frost-withered weeds, so the birds hurtled up, leveled off so that they were head high, and—all twenty of them—started for the thicket. I was shooting a 12-gauge auto-loader, a gun I fancied was just the ticket for all my hunting forever (shows what you know at seventeen), and I went to work. When the smoke cleared, I had three birds with three shots, and I carried on a litany for the next hour about how easy this quail shooting business really was.

The next few coveys caught me in their line of departure, and I missed something like eighteen shots in a row. The first flush was a freak, the birds like tin cans on a post. Subsequent coveys wised me up pronto.

On the plains, you have the further distraction—as if long-range confusion were not enough—of pheasants. The normal quail shooting scenario in that part of the world finds the shooter after pheasants, and the quail come up. Naturally, the choice of gun and load would not be the same if only one or the other species was expected.

A friend of mine, Dave Meisner of Iowa, hunts like a fanatic all season in his home state with periodic sojourns to Missouri. Dave hunts with a 20-gauge over/under bored improved cylinder/modified and high-base #7½s, simply because he admits that when the dog points—and Dave has some good ones—he's never sure what will come up. This combination is his most workable compromise. If a covey moves, Dave may switch to 8s for the singles work. I've tried this set-up, and it works.

Quail, throughout their range, are never very far from standing, permanent cover. In the South, this can mean swampland or pine stands; on the plains or in the West—such as in Oklahoma and Texas where they shoot quite a few quail—it means the thick growth found variously in plum thickets, watercourses, and stands of cactus capable of opening an artery. Once in the thick stuff, the birds behave, as indicated, like pretty fair imitations of ruffed grouse. Here is where the quick gun comes into its own.

Tradition, that shroud of myths and fact mixed up and served to upland shooters, dictates a 20-gauge gun for quail. It's hard to argue with the choice for day in and day out, from open fields to sloughs and brushy draws.

First, in most situations for most of us, the 20-gauge is lighter to carry and swing. This can mean a lot after a few miles of the knees getting lifted to the chin to get through the stuff you're hunting. Second, to most hunters, this gun is readily available; there isn't a gunmaker doing business in this country that doesn't offer a 20-gauge version of its line, and they all seem to take special pains to make sure that this gauge—often the flagship of the sales volume fleet—is nicely finished. Twenty-bore shells are easy to come by, and the loadings offered are starting to rival those of the 12-gauge. Finally, for the most part these guns are well balanced and do a dandy job on quail.

But, lest we start thinking of this or that gun as a "quail gun," let's make sure we take a look at conditions. I think the average shotgunner—and, brother, I'm nothing if not average—should examine the conditions he's going to hunt and think in terms of the gun that's effective for them.

For example, let's look at the southern hunting of bobwhites. In this situation, the ranges are normally short-covey rises at under ten yards, and the thick-cover single-bird shooting sometimes under ten *feet*. A gun that handles fast and delivers a pattern spread that will compensate for some excusably sloppy holding and still not mince a centered bird seems to work best.

Additionally, a gun with its weight centered either between the hands (at the hinge pin of a double) or slightly weight forward works better than a butt-heavy/muzzle-light gun. Let me explain.

When a covey goes up and you've positioned yourself correctly, most of the shots are going to be straightaways—birds making a direct line away from you and toward the cover they seek for escape. A gun with a weight bias toward the rear, when slammed to the shoulder during the frenzy of a covey rise, has a tendency to bounce around for a bit. On a true straightaway shot, there is no gun movement—it's a straight snap shot at what is effectively a stationary target. True, most shots will offer an angle, but only a slight one. So a gun with between-the-hands balance comes up to the shoulder and stays put when you draw down. If I had to make a choice between a gun with barrel lightness and one with stock lightness, I would choose the butt-light gun every time.

But once the birds have made cover, and the singles are pursued, things change. Quail in thick cover offer more short crossing shots, shots that have to be taken very quickly or not at all. The real expert brush shot—regardless of the species he's after—is a shooter who favors a distinct muzzle lightness in his guns. He relies upon his experience to trigger the shot at the proper time, and he is usually among the better shots of upland bird hunters. His gun would be of little value with open-field doves or pheasants crossing at the end of a brushy draw. But in the thick stuff, such a gun is deadly.

I use a gun like this on woodcock and ruffed grouse—not because

This setter is not the traditional banjo-ribbed pointer that many identify with the South, but it works like one: way out and going strong until a covey is hit, and then the dog holds until the next Ice Age. The gun, a straight-gripped 20 of five-and-a-half pounds, is quick on these birds.

I'm a great shot, but because the great shots use them. (Maybe someone will confuse me with a good shot.) But with quail, you can't
always use it. In the South you can get, variously, some fairly open
covey shooting followed by thick-cover singles work, the bread-and-
butter of quail gunning. The gun that does one well doesn't do the
other so hot. So, improvise.

I've got a 20-gauge double I use that is muzzle-light. Its twenty-
five-inch barrels handle like a flash in the puckerbrush, but I have a
tendency either to lag or overswing on crossing birds in the open, and
when I stab that gun to my shoulder for a bird heading straight away
in the open, I bounce the barrels like the blip on an oscilloscope.

To get around this problem, I use lead tape to add weight to the
barrels—to change the balance to more weight-forward—for shooting
in the open. When I go into the thick cover after the singles, I just strip
off the tape—which is placed underneath, half-way between the end
of the forend and the muzzles—and I'm back to a muzzle-light piece
for the snap shooting quail offer in the brush.

Now, if you try this technique, remember to give the gun a few
practice swings before you head in to reacquaint yourself with the
new feel of the gun, and be sure to place the weight in the same place
every time or you'll never familiarize yourself with the gun. I got this
idea from a pal I play golf with who changes the feel of his irons with
tape. He may make five or six weight/balance changes in a round of
golf, and he says he's just "fine-tuning" his clubs for the shots offered.
Since he beats the snot out of me every round, I can't argue with his
method.

Chokes are fairly easy for the southern hunting: as open as you
can get them. This is the place for skeet/skeet, cylinder/skeet, or cylin-
der/improved cylinder. The shots—even in the open—are likely to be
short, and you need all the pattern you can get in the brush. With
such open borings, you'll need small shot to densify the pattern. An
ounce of shot in #8 or #9 is a good choice, perhaps one of each in the
tubes of a double. Late in the season, tighten down to improved
cylinder/modified.

The repeating gun, either a pump or an auto, used for southern
hunting should be bored no tighter than improved cylinder, and the
barrel should be no longer than twenty-six inches—a good idea is
having the barrel lopped to twenty-three or twenty-four inches and
choke tubes installed. That way, if you need to change things around a
bit, you have the flexibility.

But it's been my experience that the repeating gun just does not
possess the handling characteristics of a lively double, and with the

Now the shooting gets tough. Quail buzz out and through such cover quickly, and you have to be alert. Shooting is an instinctive thing here, and the barrel-light gun has an advantage.

cost of even a low-grade auto, a quail hunter can get into a used double that will make his heart sing.

Now, because of the requirements of a southern quail gun, you can pick your gauge. The 20 probably comes the closest to fulfilling the need, but a light 12 shooting an ounce or one-and-one-eighth ounces of shot can do the trick, too. The 16-gauge was for years the choice of the landed southern gentry because of the way it handles an ounce of shot, and some still swear by this dinosaur among shotguns. A trip to the bayou country will still acquaint you with the names Parker, L. C. Smith, Ansley H. Fox, and others, and in these old classics, there are a lot of 16s.

As far as weight—being less important than balance—it's up to you. How strong are you? Slightly built shooters may feel that six pounds is plenty—an ex–football tackle may swing a seven-and-a-half-pound gun like a wand. Just remember, a muzzle-light gun is going to feel lighter overall than a muzzle-heavy gun even if they are the same weight, because your strong hand is lifting for only a short distance the greatest concentration of weight to your face. If you're right-handed and you're shooting a gun with the weight distribution well forward, your extended, weaker left hand has to do most of the work. This slows everything down, but only slightly.

Another thing about a gun that has the weight up front: It may be hard to stop and thus smoother once you get it going, but what you don't hear very often is that sometimes you just can't get it going in the first place—like in a tight spot in the cover. If all your shooting is in such places, use a muzzle-light gun.

On the plains, where shots are longer, wind is a factor—both in what it does to birds and to shot strings—and the thick-cover shooting is less thick than in the South; so a different gun is called for. Here you need more choke. I think an ounce of shot is still enough in most cases, but I've had days when I shot short-magnum 20s in the tight barrel. Late in the season, birds jump wilder and fly faster as they gain strength heading into the winter. You have to compensate.

On the plains, I like a gun with a longer barrel. Perfectly, twenty-eight-inch barrels in a double, but with the weight still pretty much between the hands, although a weight-forward bias is okay here, and—if it's slight—you won't have to change things chasing thick-cover singles.

Chokes for plains quail can be improved cylinder/modified, improved cylinder/full, or—in a single-barreled gun—a loose modified, say something that patterns fifty percent at the pattern board. I like a 20 bored IC/Full, because the speed of a covey means that if my first shot is at twenty yards, my second shot is likely to come at thirty-five yards, especially if the birds cut with the wind—and they almost always do.

Lots of times, especially when there's a chance for pheasants, I'll carry a light 12-gauge bored improved cylinder/modified. Since shot load and choke matter more—to me anyway—than gauge, this light 12 fulfills the needs of a plains quail gun, especially when pheasants remain a distinct possibility. There are a number of delightful 12-gauge loads in light weight—an ounce or one-and-one-eighth ounces—quail-gathering sizes of from #7½–#8 that can be used with such a gun.

The problem is finding a gun like this—you aren't going to get one from too many American makers, the exception at this writing being the Browning Sidelock in 12 gauge. This gun is rated at a little over six-and-a-half pounds, but the ones I've handled were all lighter than that. The stock has a little too much drop for my taste, but I shoot a trap stock height, and a little work can make this gun fit anyone. This gun is a close approximation of a sidelock British game gun in weight and feel. If you shoot a 12 or would like to because of the versatility, rest assured that there are guns around the weight of 20s, and the shot-load offerings for them also approximate the 20. And you have the flexibility to go heavier for other game without the loss of pattern performance that plagues a 20-gauge when you stick a Roman candle load through a small muzzle.

Western Quail

Until now, I've talked mainly about bobwhite hunting, and with pretty good reason: They are by far the most popular and the most widely distributed. But there are other birds that are called quail that regularly give hunters fits because of their predisposition toward running: the western quail.

Of these, the beautiful Mearns quail, the rarest of the bunch, is also the most civilized, behaving much like the bobwhite when it comes to holding for a dog and flushing as a covey in the traditional sense.

However, this quail is a southwestern bird, haunting Mexico, Arizona, New Mexico, and Texas. Unlike the desert quail cousins he has nearby, the Mearns prefers the moister borders and cooler uplands near the desert. He probably runs a bit more than a bob, but nowhere near the track-star gymnastics of the other, desert quails.

The gun I've described for the bobwhite on the plains will do you well on Mearns quail, in the unlikely event you ever hunt them. There are not that many of them, and each bird taken is a real trophy. They usually hang out in coveys of a dozen birds, and I'd highly recommend that anyone who hunts Mearns think only of hunting the covey rises, leaving the singles alone to regroup. With small coveys—of any of the quails—overshooting is a real danger. The birds covey up for protection, a behavioral adaptation. Removing a number of the birds from a covey eliminates too many important sets of eyes and ears, and opens the birds up to predation. In many states, quail hunting is forbidden by law to extend past a certain hour in the afternoon, say 4:00. This gives the birds a chance to find each other, regroup, and get settled in for the night. Chasing singles until dark makes no moral or ethical sense. Certainly it makes no sense if you plan ever to hunt the birds again—it's nice to know where you can locate a covey if you want one.

As harsh weather comes on, any of the quails pick up stragglers from other coveys that have been decimated by predation and weather, and in the spring these birds pair off and nest, starting new coveys. They've got it down to a science.

When it comes to foot speed, the Jesse Owens of the quail clan is the scaled quail. Also called the "cottontop" or "blue quail," these birds can pick them up and lay them down. And they have a tendency to do it in big bunches, with a typical covey of blues about twice the size of those bobs.

The way to get shooting at scalies is to find a gang of them and run like hell. The first flush of the covey will come at extreme range, and if you're smart, you'll hold your fire, because the hunting is only starting. Now, with the covey scattered, you start hunting the singles and the twos and threes that have headed for the thick stuff, which can cause you to make a post-hunt trip to the blood bank for a withdrawal.

The scalie comes off the ground fairly high and normally farther out than you'd think, so a gun that holds tight is a good choice. At least one barrel of a double should be modified, and a repeater bored this way is good, too—you can always wait out a close flusher.

Dogs that have been broken on bobwhites will have a tough time hunting scaled quail. On the one hand, you want the dog maybe to give you a hand scattering a covey; later, you'll ask him to be a good doggie and hold the birds in the classic style. Most dogs can't handle both, so the scaled quail hunter does his own bird busting while the dog stands there with his mouth open, his suspicions about your sanity finally, after these many years, confirmed.

The plains quail gun can also do you some good work on another runner: the Gambel's quail. Although a little less of a runner than the scaled quail, this one legs it and is a faster flyer, I think. Rooting singles from a busted covey out of thick cover can test your quick swing and fast handling. I think partly because of the deceptive distances of the desert air, both Gambel's and scaled quail are shot behind; they're farther out there than they look, and they're moving faster to boot.

To me, the valley or California quail is the most nerve-wracking to hunt because he gathers in huge coveys that run ahead of you just out of shotgun range. Most coveys, sad to say, get scattered by hunters who, frustrated with the running gambit, ground-pound a few. These birds also, when scattered, seem to disappear in the thickets of cactus and brush. I will not walk across the street for all the Gambel's quail in the world. If you insist on hunting them, use a gun that carries light—you'll need it.

The mountain quail is the biggest of the quail, and has some of the same running habits. The speciation of these birds and their habitats have imprinted the running habit in them pretty good, and aside from the bob and the Mearns, it is rare when you get shooting at birds you haven't had to chase a bit first. Hunting these birds is a sport for the young of heart—speaking physiologically, now—and leg; by the time the birds come up and your gun is waving around in the air, the birds can put some distance between them and you. I'd say, go light with the gun, and go tight with the choke: light and tight.

5

Pheasants

When it comes to pheasants in this decade—and for the rest of this century—there's good news and there's bad news. The good news is that there are probably going to be more of these birds than there have been for a number of years; the bad news is they're going to be just as hard to get in the air and kill as they always were.

In December 1985, the president signed into law the comprehensive Farm Bill, which contained a number of things for farmers, including a provision to take out of production a large amount of acreage designated as "highly erodible" land. Soil erosion is a big problem across the grain belt and elsewhere on this continent, and this provision served to address that problem. First, the provision would cut down on the farming of acreage that was subject to abnormal amounts of wind and water erosion. In Iowa, for example, it's been estimated that for every bushel of corn produced, a bushel of topsoil was also lost.

Soil experts say that this valuable topsoil—the "A horizon" of a soil profile—takes years to build up and that the prairie grasses that lived, died, decayed, and enriched the soil are no longer found, thus the topsoil in this country is a finite resource. Someday, unless we do something, it will be gone and with it the ability to feed most of the world—and all of us Americans.

Well, the Farm Bill's provision removing this land from production also served to reduce the number of and amount of crops being dumped onto a glutted and depressed market, thus farmers could actually make a living from what they grew if acreage were limited.

How much land out of production? Something in the neighborhood of forty-five million acres, and for ten to fifteen years. Now, fellow pheasant hunters, are the light bulbs going on? As you read this, the first acres taken out of production under this provision are starting to be used by pheasants as nesting habitat; later, as the vegetation on these previously barren acres rejuvenates, the same land will provide winter sheltering cover. Interestingly, this Conservation Reserve provision corresponds with the Conservation Reserve section of the old Soil Bank program of the 1950s and 1960s with one important difference: The Farm Bill lands are larger. By comparison, the Soil Bank program had at one time a maximum of twenty-eight million acres set aside at any one time. This could get ugly for the home team—us.

Here's an example: As of September 1, 1986, less than a year after the bill was passed, Iowa had already enrolled 385,000 acres in the program for ten years. The Iowa Department of Natural Resources is predicting: "The future for pheasants and quail in Iowa is looking better than it has for many years."

Now, we could be looking at a return to the glory days of the 1950s under this program, and—at the least—it couldn't hurt. So be prepared—we may be turning back into a nation of pheasant hunters before too long.

The problem that pheasant hunters constantly face is one of simply getting a shot. Pheasants run. They run like they're thieves with your TV tucked under their wings, and they fly as a last resort. In the past, as today, getting a limit of pheasants, or even a shot, was a numbers game. If there were ten roosters on a farm, and eight slickered you, then you had a sporting chance at only two. If, however, there are fifty roosters on a farm, and the same eighty percent outran you, that still leaves you with a chance at ten. I think that pheasants don't run any more now than they did when I was a kid; instead, I think they are just fewer in number. After all, most of a pheasant's

The old: the rooster pheasant, more legs than wings, more brains and savvy than anything else. A Chinese import, this bird has found a niche in America but is totally dependent on farming practices that will help him.

predators, with the exception of humans, are defeated ultimately by its flight. The fox, the cat, the coyote, the skunk, the raccoon, the weasel, and a lot of others are ground-bound, and when running fails to discourage them, the pheasant simply lifts into the air and is gone. We are *not* breeding a generation of runners by shooting the flyers — I've been hearing that one for thirty years.

If shooting flyers meant the runners were alive and well to reproduce others with the running strain in them, then we should never have any traffic accidents because we've killed off the accident-prone drivers, leaving only safe drivers as brood stock, right? Well, it doesn't work for pheasants either. And the fact is, it takes thousands of generations before a behavioral adaptation like running becomes a genetic fact. We haven't had that much time trimming flyers from the gene pool yet.

So the problem becomes getting pheasants into the air and then making the shot once we do. Pheasants are birds of the waste places. They need cover for nesting — young, low cover is best — and they need cover for protection from predators and the weather, and they need this cover — with food either in it or very near to it — in direct proportion to the stresses of weather and predation. In other words, if there are a lot of predators and there's a run of really bad winters, then the birds need superb cover. In milder winters, which happen periodically, they can make do with a little less protection.

Now, in today's farming practices, in order to make a buck the farmer has to farm a lot of land. He has to do it efficiently, and he has to do it on a large scale. Sure, there aren't many Mom and Pop farms anymore, but there aren't any Mom and Pop auto plants or silicon chip laboratories, either. Farming's not that much different.

Because of this, farmers have had to get with it, they've had to join the twentieth century, bless 'em. This means big machinery, herbi-

The new: a blackneck pheasant. Capable of living in more marginal habitat than the ringneck, he even roosts in trees and fills a niche in cover that ringnecks disdain. Hybrids of these birds with ringnecks may be the key to the future in some states. Photo courtesy of Michigan DNR.

cides, pesticides, and fields with the fencelines pulled up so that those big machines can get a good, long run at those pesticided, herbicided fields. If you're looking for nice wide fencerows holding pheasants, buy a Bob Abbett painting.

Instead, the places holding pheasants these days are the places where farming isn't efficient, places where the farmer has figured that he's best off just letting it be. Maybe it's a place too wet during planting and harvest time; maybe it's a woodlot he wants to save; maybe the angle of the slope is such that his jillion-dollar tractor will tip over if he gets too close; maybe it's a creekbed or slough that he doesn't want anything to do with. In any event, these are the places our farmer friend stays away from, and these are the places that the pheasants gravitate to.

So hunting pheasants these days is a matter of hunting the permanent cover that is there year-around, hunting the areas that are providing the bird with food, cover from the weather, and shelter from his predators. These are the places you go after him, not in the standing corn where he runs like a thief, not the stubble fields where he ventures only briefly if at all, and not in those laughable excuses for fencerows.

Getting a pheasant into the air requires the planning and strategy

A late-season bird takes to the air. Getting near winter pheasants is tough, unless there is wind to cover your noise. The field of grass has been there for several years, typical of the type of cover these birds require when the winter winds blow.

of a military campaign, for the pheasant is the smartest of all the upland gamebirds. Heavy praise? Well, pheasants come from Asia, where they have lived next to humans since they both swung down from their respective trees. Where the wild turkey is super-cautious, the Canada goose is super-wary, and the ruffed grouse is super-fast, the pheasant is just super-smart, and that's it.

You've got to go at him by eliminating his options. He'll run first, and you really can't stop him from running. Instead, you've got to force him to run toward a place of your choosing where he can't run any more and has to fly. You've got to work his cover thoroughly and slowly so that he can't slip back around you. You've got to position your people so that someone will have a shot when he clatters into the air, and you've got to hit him hard and sometimes repeatedly to bring him in. And you've got to use a good dog and give that dog every advantage by using your head so that he can use his nose.

For starters, the ringneck of today is a bird that wises up in a hurry. Most of the birds that are going to absorb chilled 6s in their lifetimes are going to do so during the first hour of the first day of their first season. After that, they become really smart birds, and your chance of getting them drops like a head-shot dove. In some states, it's estimated that the first hour's kill accounts for more than half of the birds that will be shot all season. Now, there isn't a slaughter, but just a bunch of uneducated birds that have been ganged up on. The survivors wise up pronto, and they stay wise their entire lives.

Looking for birds in roosting cover the first part of the morning—say just at legal shooting time—makes sense. But that roosting cover—normally grass fields that have been around for a couple of years—should be near feed and near good escape cover such as creekbeds and brushy draws.

Early in the season, try farm terraces. These are unlevel spots between level fields that farmers have found cannot be farmed without high erosion losses, so they are left alone. Sometimes these are quite thick, but usually they are just growing up in high grass. Later in the season, as weather takes its toll, these terraces are flattened and become unuseable as pheasant habitat, and they're best forgotten.

Creekbeds are a good bet because they usually have a long history of not being disturbed. Trees, thick brush, blackberry canes, and a lot of other things have grown up there, and the birds will use these spots year after year. Likewise, ditches and the attendant cover they provide are likely spots, as are railroad lines that are no longer used. In many places, the tracks and ties have been pulled up and carted away, but the grades remain. These lines were once the lifeblood of the plains,

A rooster pheasant, a stubble field, and a full-choked auto-loader. Jim Pruitt, who owns Trapper Jim's Hunt Club in Kingston, Michigan, shows off for his dog. Sadly, such days of "easy" shooting are now long gone.

putting farmers in touch with markets in the East and bringing in life necessities to places like Iowa, Nebraska, Kansas, and South Dakota—the premier pheasant states. Today, that's not nearly the case, and these spur lines have grown up into what is often good pheasant habitat. The lines, like creekbeds, may run for miles through farm country, and thus they put the birds close to feed.

Wherever you choose to hunt, make sure that you take away the birds' best defense—running. The best way to do that is to push the running pheasants ahead of you to an area where they cannot run, where they'll have to sit tight and hope that you'll pass them by. With farm terraces, this means working the cover toward an open field, one that has been plowed or picked, in which cover is thin and the birds will feel exposed and thus flush. With creekbeds, pushing them toward a road or farm lane works. But what works better here — as it does with railroad rights-of-way — is the old block and drive.

In the block and drive, the pheasants are pushed by some hunters until they encounter other hunters who are waiting at a natural escape point; they usually get the shooting when the birds, trapped, take wing. Anyone who spent his early years waiting at the end of a cornfield knows the thrill of having blocked a rooster that suddenly springs into the air almost at your feet. It's the same technique, only used in permanent cover.

What you want to do is send someone — or two — ahead of the main party. The main party, which may be one man and a good dog, then pushes the cover slowly, herding the unseen, running birds toward the blockers. When the birds encounter the blockers, they are likely to flush. Surprised, they figure they're surrounded and take off, which is what you want, naturally.

But the trick is to get the blockers into position as silently as possible. The blockers may have to use their cars or make long circular treks on foot to get into position. What you do *not* want is the blockers passing through or even near any of the places where the drive is going to take place. You don't want the birds to know anything's up. This means getting out of the car quietly, no talking, and silent movements.

Once the drivers and blockers are in position, the drive begins — preferably into the wind to mask the noise of the drivers, thus keeping the birds ahead of you, but as close as possible, and also to give your dog a chance to work the wind.

On long creekbeds and on railroad grades, try leapfrogging the blockers ahead two hundred yards, driving that two hundred yards, and then leapfrogging the blockers ahead another two hundred yards — taking the long, narrow cover a chunk at a time, in other words.

In the East, pheasant hunting is more of a pockets-of-cover proposition, waste places that will hold a bird or two, and the cover and hunting conditions are more reminiscent of ruffed grouse hunting than pheasant shooting. Here the birds may be almost full-time residents of woodlots or brushy draws that resemble good woodcock cover. In fact, in Michigan I've shot rooster pheasants and woodcock from the same streamside alder thickets on the same day, the pheasants heading for the cover that was available.

Dogs for pheasant hunting can be as diverse as farm collies and blooded setters, but day in and day out, the springer spaniel and the Labrador retriever are going to be the best bets. Working as flushing dogs, these breeds very closely approximate the hunting actions of a fox or coyote in that they trail and chase a pheasant so that he has to take flight to save his precious carcass. The springer is probably the best, having been bred for many years specifically for pheasant hunting. The Lab, a breed that readily forsakes the duck blind for the thick stuff, has a similar hunting style and brings with it as well the important retrieving skills and instincts that can make the difference between a hit bird and a bagged bird. In fact, any dog that will retrieve is worth taking along, even if the mutt only follows at heel until a bird is shot before he goes into action.

My pal Chuck Lichon has a Lab who loves pheasant hunting, and I've never seen her lose a downed bird. She isn't stylish to the eye of a pointing-dog man, but so what? She finds birds, roots them into the air, and fetches them in when Charlie gets lucky. That's about all you can ask.

For the pointing breeds, a lot can be said for the German shorthair and any of the versatile breeds of dogs—the pudelpointer, the German wirehair, and the like. Bred in Europe for a wide variety of game species—everything from ducks to woodchucks, it seems—these dogs will point, but they'll also trail, and they are death on wingtipped roosters. Dave Meisner of Iowa—whom I'd classify as a pheasant-hunting expert—owns and swears by his wirehair, Max. I've hunted with the breed, and I like 'em. But boy, are they ugly.

A pheasant dog has to be able to work close, close enough so that if he bumps a bird or gets it into the air, it will be within gun range. With many bird species, I don't think enough owners have enough confidence in their dogs to allow them to work at a range that's more natural for them; owners prefer to keep them close. But with pheasants, no pointing breed is going to handle all his birds all the time and wait for you to come strolling up to sack the meat. So the dog has to keep his wits about him, and he also has to stay close.

Working cover so that the dog gets the wind serves the twofold advantage of masking your sound and bringing scent to your dog, as I've mentioned. That's another reason why drives have to be planned. Pheasants are bad enough on a dog without the added encumbrance of a wind at his back. Plus, pheasants will usually flush into the wind but quickly cut with it, so a bird pushed with the wind will usually flush long, flush going away, and flush with the wind carrying him. All of these things conspire to rob you of a decent chance for a clean kill.

My setter, Jess, loves to hunt pheasants. The scent of these big birds is so strong that she—after early-season bouts with grouse and woodcock—has a tendency at first to point them way too far off, and until we've hunted a few days, she won't break point and relocate a running bird the way I'd like. Then, when we switch back to grouse, she often bumps the first few by being *too* bold and aggressive. The man who hunts a lot of species of birds with one dog constantly fights this problem, but it's a price we pay for loving one mutt. Thankfully, as she gets older (she's heading into her fifth season), she makes the transitions faster. Experience, I guess.

One trick you hear about is the dog that will circle a running bird and pin it by coming back on it—a variation of the block and drive, with the dog being its own driver and blocker. I've seen it done, and my dog does it once in a while when she's in the mood. But it's a scam they have to learn on their own, because you can't train them to do it. It's most often pulled on pheasants, but Jess does it more on ruffed grouse. I gave up trying to figure out why.

The 1985 Farm Bill should make even better the states that harbor good populations of pheasants. These states all have vast acreage into agricultural land, also this is where farmers are really hurting and are more likely to take advantage of the economic incentives the bill offers.

For years, South Dakota was the pheasant capital of the world, then Nebraska led the nation in birds killed. Later, Iowa came on strong. Now, many reports indicate that Kansas is a real comer. In most of these states, the seasons run well into the winter, making the birds of late season a challenge. The out-of-staters, especially those from the East, have a number of choices about where to go, and a letter to the game departments of any of these states will entitle you to a nifty pack of information about seasons, prospects, lodging, costs, where-to-hunt tips such as managed areas, and so forth. For many easterners, the trip west for pheasants each year is a ritual.

Having taught my own two sons at an early age the intricacies and rewards of playing hookey from school, we make an annual event of this November pheasant hunt. In the Great Lakes states, where I live, most of the shooting for other species is about done when the seasons open on the plains, so along about the opener of the Iowa (or Nebraska or South Dakota) season, we're gone. When I was a kid, my father and I made regular trips to Nebraska for pheasants and quail, and the habit has held on.

Shooting a pheasant is not a tough proposition compared with some other bird hunting that places an emphasis and premium on marksmanship. For example, a woodcock gives you all you can handle most days, but if you sprinkle him even lightly with fine shot, he's

Remember your first bird? Author's son Chris with a fat winter rooster taken with his single-barrel 20, with a tight choke to compensate for a young inexperienced shooter's lack of speed. Later on, the youngsters we hunt with will beat us to the draw and start asking for expensive guns!

yours. He doesn't really run, he can't take much hitting, and he's altogether a gentlemanly bird. Not the ringneck. This character saves some of his slimiest tricks for when he's down, giving dogs twitches and ruining your day if he gets away. So the ticket is to kill him in the air. *Pow! Whack!* Deader 'n a smelt! That's what you want. But it ain't easy.

The typical shot at a pheasant, under the average conditions, tends toward the longish side. On the plains, where distances are easy to misjudge anyway, shots are longer than back East where you have better reference points, trees and things. And, since the seasons open late on pheasants, usually, you have a heavily feathered, fat-ladened bird, one that can take the shock of big loads without coming down dead.

So the ticket for pheasants is a gun that will deliver the maximum amount of shot you can lay into a bird, and will do it quickly. Because in some instances, like a bird that's got a little time to get moving with a wind, he can be fast.

Normally a pheasant flushes fairly straight up, and his long tail, vibrating behind him, makes you misjudge where the important parts

Tracks show where these two winter hunters passed by a skulking cock pheasant, but the setter wasn't fooled. In the winter before a storm, birds often hold well for a pointing dog. Within eight hours of the time this photo was taken, a snowfall of six inches moved in.

are, the parts with eyes and ears and white rings. And he is often cackling at you, which, translated, comes out in a bunch of four-letter words, pheasant-style.

All of this conspires to make you shoot at the middle of a pheasant. This works great on grouse and quail and other birds, but a pheasant is about one-third air surrounded by feathers, and another third non-vital bone and gristle. He's only one-third vital area, and that third is located up front where he can keep an eye on things.

Because he's coming straight up, and because he looks like he's barely moving, comparatively speaking, we have a tendency to shoot him toward the rear end. A going-away pheasant offers us only the rear-end shot, a place that will give you the knock-down but not the knock-out.

To kill a pheasant dead in the air, you have to hit him at decent range for the choke and load you're using, you have to hit him in the forward third of the body—ahead of the wing joints—and you have to put several—at least four—shots in the vitals. If you really want him, you'll have to break a wing, too.

At home, when I clean gamebirds, I have a variety of tools. I use a short little filet knife, made from a longer one I broke, to clean woodcock and quail. I use a standard pocket folding knife for cleaning ruffed grouse. For pheasants, I take off the head, feet, and wings with a hatchet and a chopping block. Those parts are just too tough to handle easily any other way. There's a message there, and it has to do with shooting them—and killing them.

This is no place for your dainty small bores. This is big gauge, big shot, tight choke shooting. My sons use 20-gauge doubles, but their guns are chambered for three-inch magnum shells. There is not a lot of shooting at pheasants. Even on a good day with some misses thrown in, you'll likely shoot fewer than half a dozen times, and a box of shells will probably last you all season. Because of this, don't worry about getting recoil shy—it won't happen. Not with pheasants. The boys are likely to shoot a three-inch #6 or #4—or even a tight-patterning #4 steel in their left barrel. If you want to shoot a 20, fine. Just make sure that at least one barrel is full or can be made to pattern full by choosing—and patterning—the right load.

By far, the 12-gauge is the number one choice of most pheasant hunters, with autos and pumps long considered the standard. The Model 12 Winchester, the Remington 870, and the Ithaca 37 probably are the favored pumps, while the Remington 1100 and Browning Auto 5 are a couple of the top choices among the auto-loaders. Of these, the

Remingtons probably account for most of the pheasants this country's gunners shoot each fall.

Some folks still prefer the double. In pheasant shooting, the over/under is a good choice; you're likely to have a clear background where the single sighting plane of an O/U really comes into its own.

Still, others like a side-by-side. I like them for everything, and I use them on pheasants. I've got two that I especially like. The first is a 12-gauge bored tight improved cylinder and improved modified, and the other is a light 12 bore French game gun with twenty-eight-inch barrels bored tight IC and full. The first 12 has twenty-five-inch barrels and weighs only a shade over six pounds. I take that gun when it looks like a lot of my shooting will be in thick cover. The French gun is my plains gun, the one I use on the prairies for a variety of game, pheasants among them.

These guns, as yours should be, are stocked very straight—not much drop at all. This does two things: It throws the recoil from fairly heavy loads straight back rather than up (into your face) and back, and it also places the shot pattern high. How high? I'd say that if your

The shooter of the WWII generation favors the "Perfect Repeater," a Winchester Model 12 for his pheasant work . . .

. . . while this 1980's shooter—the author—goes with a light 12-gauge for the thick cover today's birds favor. In either case, pheasants have to be hit hard, so the 12 is the most common choice.

point of aim is covered by the bottom third of your shot pattern at forty yards, you're about right. Pheasants seem to jump almost straight up, as I've mentioned, and the rising target is usually missed behind. A high-shooting gun throws the charge up a bit and into the vitals of a bird—that forward third we should be shooting at.

On plains birds, I like a long sighting plane; that's why I use twenty-eight-inch barrels a lot out West. But longer barrels will give you a view of more barrel when you mount the gun than will, say, twenty-five-inch barrels. Short barrels shoot a little higher than long barrels, and your gun has to be stocked accordingly.

Also, the pheasant gun shouldn't weigh a lot—anything over seven-and-a-half pounds is probably too much, unless you pay for your hunting trips by winning arm-wrestling tournaments. A light gun carries easier, and you won't be shooting enough to get the flinchies, as I said. But there shouldn't be the lightness of a quail gun because you'll be shooting big loads.

If the gun balances between the hands—at the hinge pin of a double—you're fine. If anything, a little weight forward would help. Short barrels are easy to stop in the open—not so easy to stop in the brush where you're usually just taking a stab at a flurry of wings and rarely get a chance for a proper swing. The gun I use on grouse and woodcock will take pheasants in the brush, but in the open, I'm lost. That gun is balanced to be muzzle-light, and mostly I miss open pheasants with it.

Tight chokes allow you to take the long shot once in a while, and they also allow you to wait out a close-flushing bird and drop him once the pattern opens a bit. This trick—on any gamebird—is what marks the experienced and "finished" wingshot. One day you'll just find yourself saying: "Ah, a grouse/pheasant/woodcock/quail. I see that the bird has chosen an escape route that will force it to cover thirty-five yards of open ground before cover can shield it. Since the bird is now six yards from my muzzles, and since this gun is bored to print its best patterns at twenty-five yards, I shall wait until the bird has advanced toward the cover another eighteen yards and then shoot." Well, something like that, and a helluva lot faster, but come the day when it happens, pat yourself on the back, lad. You're there.

With pheasants, placing yourself so that you don't have to shoot right at the stern of a rooster will result in more first-shot kills. Approach your dog from the side if he's pointing, or place a partner a distance away if a flushing breed is cutting figures in the weeds; one of you will get a chance at the exposed front end of a pheasant, the area where the bird carries its life.

High-velocity loads are called for here. In 12-gauge, one-and-a-quarter ounces of #5 or #6 shot pushed by three-and-a-quarter drams of powder is good, potent medicine for these birds, and corresponding loads in 16- or 20-gauge should suffice as well—maximum or near maximum loads.

In this book, it seems like I've turned into a real promoter of the 16, and I guess I have. I'd like to see a turnaround in this country in that gauge's popularity. Maybe it'll happen. But, with pheasants, I can see no difference between a 16 and a 12—but I can see a big difference between a 12 and a 20. Again, if you want to *kill* pheasants, leave your small bores home.

So for pheasants, here goes: a 12 or a 16 or a three-inch 20; straight, high-shooting stock; weight either between the hands or forward; chokes either modified on a repeating gun or tight improved cylinder and modified on a double or, better yet, one of the barrels full choke on a double; weight under seven-and-a-half pounds, and closer to six-and-a-half is better.

6

Other Birds

Chukars

Chukars, like pheasants, are an import that worked out in this country because they occupied an empty niche in the ecosystem. In this case, the niche is in some of the most desolate terrain found on this or any other nearby planet—the high rugged uplands of the dry western mountain ranges.

The chukar, an Asian import, took to things nicely after its introduction into this country in the 1930s. There were some early failures until the game department people got it through their skulls that the birds actually *liked* the semi-arid lands and didn't want anything to do with the eastern United States.

The bird is bigger than a quail and smaller than a grouse and has some unusual habits. First, it likes to run—uphill. The best way to get a chukar to fly is to get above him and come at him and his cronies from above. This not only is easier, once you get above the birds, it's also more effective. Getting above the birds, however, is not easy.

The chukar, another import that has done well, is at his best in the arid highlands of the West.

Sometimes, a hard switchback road grade will place you above areas that chukars are using, and they are nice enough to call to let you know they're there. But most often, it's a matter of trudging up the rimrock and then walking parallel for a while before coming back down through fresh country. Most hunts are more like military maneuvers because they have to be plotted carefully; you don't just walk out and chase chukars up unless you're a whole lot younger than I am.

Chukars have a tendency to dive downhill when flushed, and, if your shooting is in a boulder-strewn area, they can be very fast and tricky. Early on, some shooters started to look at birds in hand for feather patterns that would repel shot, the birds were that hard to hit.

Since the first open season on chukars was in 1955, we don't exactly have what you'd call a chukar "tradition" in this country. So the birds are often overlooked or are taken as a sidelight to western quail gunning. But they are good to eat, I think, and are worthy targets. Most places, the bag limits are high, and if you get into the birds after a fairly rainy spring and summer, their numbers can be staggering.

But dry years concentrate them near water and the attendant cover. Finding birds then is a hit-or-miss proposition only—they are either there or they aren't.

A chukar dog rests in a stream after climbing rimrock all morning. Chukars can drive a good dog wild, because they just won't hold very well.

Chukars aren't exceptionally hard to hit. In fact, they are standard game on eastern shooting preserves where they resemble quail in the way they hold for a dog and fly. But just as a grouse isn't a legend in an open field, a grass-field chukar is a big zero in my book. It's his habitat that makes him what he is.

Chukar guns had better be light, because here is really a case of foot-pounds vs. blood pressure. I like a double with unusual gradients of choke—like tight improved cylinder and full. The second shot on chukars is usually a long one. A gun of six pounds is about right, maybe more if you're in shape, but not much more.

And, although I've never tried it, I think a gun that shoots a little low could help with birds diving over the edge of rimrock or bluffs; these are not the usual upland target, which is typically rising. Even in level, straightaway flight, the bird always seems low to me. Others with more experience may disagree.

I think any gun that can throw an ounce of shot is probably okay, although one-and-one-eighth ounces would be better for second shots. There is not much shooting over classic points here; it takes a special dog to handle chukars, even those from a scattered covey. I've never hunted with a dog that could do it, but one that will retrieve saves years on your legs each season. Watch him, though, because chukar country, like old Texas, is great for men and horses, but hell on women and dogs.

Sage Grouse

Sage grouse—sage hens to many—are about the biggest of all true upland game, not counting turkeys (and I don't count them because they are hunted more like big game). A big male grouse may go over five pounds, and that's a lot for a bird. Birds are built light for flight; so, when compared with a five-pound mammal are more dense per pound—the big grouse is a real handful.

Hens are pretty stupid where they haven't been hunted much or early in the season when the young are experiencing their first dose of hostilities. The young ones, by the way, are the best eating. Often, when a crowd of hens gets up, you can pick out the young, small birds and selectively take them.

Sage hens prefer the sagebrush-infested draws where water is available, and simply working a draw toward the source of water, such

Author with a fat sage grouse taken with a 20-gauge double. Although the birds are big, they get up underfoot—most of the time—and allow shot placement in the head and neck area. But day in and day out, a 12-gauge is probably better.

as a stock tank, is usually enough. There are many empty acres in sage grouse country, and only a few that hold birds. But those few acres can be hot. In wet years, the birds can be scattered more uniformly. Then, even though the population is up, it can actually get harder to take birds because they can't easily be located in concentrated numbers.

Several years ago, I was hunting antelope in Wyoming at the Dube Outfitters out of Buffalo. I wanted to hunt hens, but they made me plug an antelope first, which I did after an exciting stalk and a lucky shot. The next day, we headed over the Bighorn Mountains and hunted outside of Ten Sleeps (love Wyoming names). The birds we found on a rancher's land had probably never seen a human before, and the first pass by Pete Dube and me got us inspected by a dozen hens that peered at us brainlessly from a yard away. We couldn't make them fly.

Now, they hadn't seen folks before, but they sure had seen coyotes, so Pete hiked back to the truck for his coyote substitute—his young Lab. Suddenly, everything changed. The birds started running, hiding, and—when the dog got close—flushing, which is what we wanted. Unlike most upland hunting, where the dog is your ally because he makes things easier, here the dog is needed to make things more sporting.

Sage grouse cover is, well, sage, especially if water is nearby.

One of my companions that trip was a man from the West who had never hunted sage hens with a dog, just potted one on the ground with a .22 when he wanted one. The sight of thirty hens in the air at once and cutting past him with the wind made a believer out of him.

Hens don't get off the ground quickly at all, even slower than a pheasant, I think. Once under speed, they provide good shooting, though, and I've been in on hunts where one man was stationed at the end of a draw and others drove the birds past him for some driven-grouse shooting of the less-than-royal style. They can really whistle under a head of steam.

I've shot sage grouse with 20s and with 12s, and a high-brass load of #4–#6 will do the trick. I suppose that the 12-gauge is the better choice, because some shooting is long if the birds have been pushed. Ahead of a pointing dog or a close-working flusher, I've had no complaints with a 20, even though it seems and sounds puny compared to the big bird and the big country he lives in.

Chaps are a good idea, and good boots are a must. In the West, almost everything picks, bites, or stabs, so your feet and legs are the parts taking most of the licking. Light clothing is best, and early in the day is best for everybody involved, including the birds and dogs. Clean the birds as soon as possible, and ice them down quickly to prevent spoilage. In many places, the season on hens opens early and that means hot weather, so dress for it.

I doubt anyone will have a shotgun stocked for sage grouse hunting; anyway, I think a high-shooting gun is in order. The birds flatten out in flight after they're in the air, but that rising flush is where most of your chances will come, and although it isn't easy, a sage hen can be missed. Under pressure and in full flight, they are missed behind, and when flushing, they are missed under (at least by me). But then, aren't they all easy to miss these ways?

I think most sage hen hunting is fun when companioned with another sport, such as big-game hunting. Sadly, I don't think these birds deserve a full-fledged trip West, but if you're out that way hunting either big game or other bird species, give them a try.

Prairie Chickens and Sharptails

Both prairie chickens and sharptails are birds of the West, primarily, and they need the open air, although the sharptail will inhabit brush land or isolated clumps of trees if they are handy. The sharptail is probably going to outlive the chicken as a species because it seems to

Cock and her prairie chicken shot in Kansas. Photo by Outdoor Images/Tom Huggler.

be more adaptable, able to use domestic grains more readily, and take advantage of man's intrusions into his home range.

The birds always are hard for me to tell apart, and if I had more experience with them, I could give you better advice. But practically, both birds reside normally in good-sized flocks, and they are difficult targets for me because they are always right on the edge of effective shotgun range. Both will run, but nothing like a pheasant, and when a crowd of them gets into the air, they can frazzle you, especially sharptails in a thicket. At such times, they can be as tricky as any brush-reared bird, if my shooting average is any indication.

In Kansas, some friends tell me, the lesser prairie chicken offers good shooting on the pass as flocks sail in, morning and evening, to feed. In Nebraska one year, my father and I got some good shooting by posting ourselves at the edge of a picked cornfield that bordered the grasslands and waiting for the birds to come in to feed. They come in low, but undulating land can make your low target suddenly high, and in those days, mostly I missed. My dad and his Model 12, partners in well-practiced sustained-lead shotgunning, always did well, and I guess that's the ticket here.

The birds are probably best taken with #6 shot fired through a modified barrel; modified and full on a double, because you can always let them get out a way before you slide one at 'em.

By the way, if you like to play the wind with your birds, deciding which direction to favor based on wind direction, forget it with these two—as an adaptation to prairie winds, the birds can fly as fast into the wind as they can with it. I know, they can't. But they can.

Hungarian Partridge

The Hun, another import, is my candidate for most frustrating bird to hunt.

First, he lives out in the open in really sparse cover—like cut wheat stubble. Second, he flushes wild if he's there at all, and the dogs have a hard time holding him, even in the rare cases when he takes up residence in some brush, especially around old houses and stock tanks. Third, he flies fast, he's small, the wind is always blowing, the sun gets in my eyes, my boots don't fit, I'm always undergunned. . . . You see how it is.

Yes, he's a challenge, this European import. And he is one of the species of upland birds that's expanding his range, pushing both south and east from his northern-plains stronghold. He likes agriculture, like the pheasant and unlike the sage hen, and to a certain extent

Tom Huggler with young North Dakota sharptail. Photo by Outdoor Images/Tom Huggler.

has filled the niche left empty when wholesale farming of the Great Plains drove the sage hen and the prairie chicken into more isolated patches. And even though both of these birds are doing better these days, the Hun is leading the league in space—his range just keeps expanding.

Bigger than a quail but smaller than a small ruffed grouse, the Hun is a tough bird. It takes a pretty good wallop to put him down for keeps, and at the extreme ranges he's often shot, a wallop is hard to deliver. So the shotgunner's answer to wallop, regardless of the bird's size, is tight choke and a lot of shot. I have shot more Huns with a 12-gauge than anything else.

The first time I hunted Huns, I can remember flushing a covey wild from a stubble field—no great trick to do that. I marked them down as they sailed toward a woodlot a mile away, and I scampered over with my dog, thinking the same strategy as for quail: scatter the covey and hunt the singles.

But, these Huns didn't scatter like quail, and the gang sailed right over or around the woodlot to the next stubble field. In the open, the Hun is at his best, and he won't handle the confines of the brush or forest well. He's safe and tricky in the open and he knows it, so that's where he stays. I got the birds up again, and they sailed off for field number one—again. I didn't follow.

Once in a while, you can get a covey to hold in cover that isn't so sparse, like around old, abandoned outbuildings. Then, a good dog will point them, but from a long, long way off. The birds will normally flush into the wind and then cut with it, sometimes coming right back past you like the Blue Angels screaming past the grandstand after an air show. Then you'll find out all about shooting behind.

I have never taken a limit of Huns; I probably never will. I'm not sure I have the willpower it takes. Maybe someday.

PART II

Guns, Gear, and Games

7

Guns

The Gauges

We've talked a lot about various guns and gauges for specific needs in the uplands. Now, let's turn our covetous eyes toward the gauges and take a look at them in terms of popularity and usefulness, with all the impartiality we can muster, which, as someone once said, ain't much.

The 12-Gauge

The 12-gauge remains the standard for upland hunting, although, as an upland gun, it doesn't have the popularity plurality that it enjoys in waterfowling.

The 12-gauge is considered the standard gauge for pheasants and the big western species, and also it is the one most often used when ranges are likely to be long. Hungarian partridge, although small birds, usually present long shots, in which the 12 excels.

The 12 handles and patterns best the big shot loads, those loads of one-and-a-quarter ounces, although for years the standard load for a 12 was one-and-one-eighth ounces of shot, the amount in a typical 12-gauge target load. The large bore diameter keeps deformation from barrel scrubbing down to a minimum compared to the same large shot load fired in a smaller gauge. The 20-gauge three-inch magnum load of one-and-a-quarter ounces of shot doesn't begin to compare with the efficiency of a high-velocity 12-gauge one-and-a-quarter-ounce load in two-and-three-quarter-inch length.

The 12-gauge, then, is a performer when it comes to ballistics. But it takes more than ballistics to make a good upland gun, so let's look a little deeper.

In England and on the European continent, more than eighty percent of the guns and the shells fired are 12s, but they are different shells and different guns than we are used to. The light game gun used there is really the equal of our American 20s in weight, ease of handling, and shot load—right around one ounce (one and one-sixteenth) being the standard 12-gauge load for most shooting conditions. But these guns are more than the 20's equal in efficiency. Because that one ounce or so of shot is being driven through a barrel much larger than a 20's, the patterns are better—more even, and the shot strings are shorter, meaning more of the shot strikes the bird at the same time, making the one-ounce 12-bore load a harder hitter than the one-ounce 20.

Luckily, this country is starting to produce one-ounce 12-gauge loads for upland game use, notably the Winchester Xpert Light Field Loads. I've shot these at grouse, woodcock, and quail, and they are deadly. But stay away from pheasants with them if the ranges are long, even in the #6 size.

The point is, the 12 is a big gun capable of shooting big loads. It seems to be at its best, however, when the weight of the gun and the shot load are both decreased, as the British have always done—at least for the last forty years or so.

If you can find a 12 that is not too bulky and heavy for you, you'll find that it offers some advantages not often mentioned or considered. For one, because of the greater shot load it delivers in most cases, the 12-gauge choke can be opened up more than the smaller gauges. A 12-gauge bored straight cylinder offers the pattern density of a 20 bored tight improved cylinder. But, of course, the cylinder is going to give several more inches of useable pattern on the edge of the pattern circle, which helps immensely with the tough shots.

When the main upland guns, the 20 and the 12, are compared

with one another, the 20 normally comes out better, the reasons given being the weight and the trim, fast-handling dynamics of the smaller gauge. I have a light 12-gauge—a little under six pounds, but with a very straight stock so recoil isn't that great. I have used this gun on occasion while grouse hunting, especially late in the season. Once, as I was coming out of the woods, I ran into a couple of fellows who were heading my way, so we walked along the two-track together and lied about our dogs, neither of which was minding us at the time.

One of the guys took note of the 12 I was carrying, and his face lit up—here I was, a blank canvas upon which he could paint the portrait of the 20-gauge over the 12. He looked at me partly in pity, partly in surprise. Surely, he said, I must know that the 20 was *the* grouse gun. Why, I asked; says he, because it is so light and fast. Nothing's as fast as a 20 in the coverts, least of all a heavy old 12 like I was carrying. I looked at his over/under 20, a good brand, but one I knew to be on the heavy side for a 20. (Aw, hell, it was a Ruger Red Label, a fine gun but one that runs closer to seven pounds than it does to six.) I told my new friend that he was right, that the 12 would never have the speed or lightness of the 20, and I handed him my gun, asking him how any man could be expected to hit a grouse with such a monstrosity. He took my gun and almost fell over. It was almost a full pound lighter than his own, his "light" 20.

I watched as the lights started to go on. Why should he carry such a heavy gun and still sacrifice some pattern and shot load when 12s like this are available, he wanted to know. Such is the shock that 20-gauge fans experience when they run up against a light 12 of the European game gun configuration.

However, such guns are rare, and a good one—a really good one, and mine isn't—is expensive. And, right now, they lack the snob appeal that is the reason many people shoot the 20 in the first place.

The other advantage the 12 has as an upland shotgun is the wide variety of loads for it. Counting the target loads that have usefulness in the uplands (for example, standard #9 skeet loads for woodcock, or hard #7½ trap loads for long-range doves), the 12's offerings are far and away the best for both flexibility in matching load to game and in availability. Additionally, the price of cheap but good 12-gauge loads is often below that of other gauges, especially if you watch for a sale someplace.

The 12 is probably the gauge most one-gun shooters would choose, but then we aren't going to be limited to one gun, right? But if we were, would it be a 12? Probably not, and in this chapter, we'll see why.

The 20-Gauge

The 20, as I've already said, is the standard gauge for upland hunters who place a premium on fast handling. Find a grouse or quail hunter, and a 20 won't be far away. And I agree: I like the 20 for quail. But I like other gauges for grouse and woodcock, and I definitely want a bigger gun for pheasants—a 16-gauge minimum, and a tight-shooting one at that.

But, the 20 is a sweetie. Interestingly, the Parker Reproduction (a real honey of a side-by-side despite its price) first came out in 20-gauge followed by 28; the third gauge due to appear, as of this writing, is the 12. The 20 is a trim gun, it is a handsome gun, but it has suffered almost too much from the praise of being "light and fast." Oftentimes, these words are not compatible. Light doesn't mean fast, always, and vice versa. If a 20 is a little heavy, it's often not considered, even though its balance and dynamics make for fast action, as with the Ruger I mentioned earlier, a heavier gun, but one that's very quick.

The 20, sadly, is not at its best when asked to do a big boy's job, like shoot big loads at big birds. The three-inch chambered 20s are versatile, they say, but the performance of the shells in that length in a 20 ranges from bad to lousy. If you have to shoot one-and-a-quarter ounces of shot, shoot a 12. Period.

But with seven-eighths ounce of shot, the standard target load, or with one ounce, the 20 is a nice performer, although not capable of some of the feats folks give it credit for.

This gauge has the allure that only nicely built, nice-looking guns can have. In its standard weight and configuration, the 20 can be carried with one hand through thick brush and still be snapped quickly into shooting position when needed. The recoil isn't much, although more than you would think when gun weight starts to nudge five-and-a-half pounds.

Now that I've said this, I'll tell you that I know some very experienced shotgunners, some whose names are household words among those who shoot, who don't even *own* a 20. They use a 28 when a small gun is called for, and a 16 or a 12 when they need more punch.

The 28-Gauge

The 28 is experiencing a rebirth for some pretty good reasons. First, this gun has a very short shot string, its shot column apparently being in harmony with its bore diameter to the point of perfection. Second, the patterns are beautiful to look at, and the load is very fast, making for a gun that performs better on game than it does on paper. Last, the recoil is light, far less than you would expect, making it pleasant to shoot all day at doves or sporting clays.

The 28-gauge has often been compared to the .410 bore, but when it really shines is when you compare it to the 20-gauge, because that's what it more closely approximates. Many grouse and woodcock hunters, both today and in the past, prefer the 28. Both Colonel H. P. Sheldon, who wrote the *Tranquillity* series, and William Harnden Foster, author of *New England Grouse Shooting*, used the 28-gauge gun for grouse, and that was when the standard load for this bore was five-eighths of an ounce. Today, the load has been increased to three-fourths of an ounce, and some handloaders put up to a full ounce in the small case, a load that was once marketed commercially.

The 28 is a fine quail gun in traditional bobwhite situations; and it makes a dandy woodcock gun as well as a dove gun—if you adequately restrict ranges on all of these birds; I don't think it's enough gun for day-in and day-out shooting at ruffed grouse for the average gunner, although the best shot I ever made on a grouse was with a 28.

I was hunting with Dave Meisner, founder of *Gun Dog* magazine, and we were working early season cover in Michigan. We were standing atop a blowdown in thick brush, resting, when a grouse flushed and went away low. The bird lifted up over a low shrub, and then dropped down behind it as they do, still carrying it fast. I drew down on the bird with my 28 just as he dropped from sight. I threw the gun high overhead, pointed it down over the top of the shrub, and fired. Pure luck, and the bird came down. The 28's light weight and toylike feeling made me do that, I guess, because I've never done it before or since, even though the birds have slickered me that way a lot since then.

The 28 is a good gun for those who are conscious of recoil, and sometimes big strappers suffer from this, especially those who have shot a lot of trap in their careers. The 28's kick seems to be light enough to diminish flinching.

If the 28 has drawbacks, they are that the offerings of loads are limited, the price of shells is quite high, and shells can't be found everywhere.

As far as weight of the gun is concerned, not everyone will agree, but I see no reason to carry a 28 that weighs more than five-and-a-half pounds. To shoot a six-and-a-half-pound 28-gauge seems to be going the opposite way that we should—a small gauge with the weight of a larger gauge. Then again, six-and-a-half pounds are very light to some people who would "throw away" a five-and-a-half-pound gun.

The other disadvantage of the 28 is that the three-quarter-ounce load means you'll have to tighten chokes down a bit over the 20's, which were tightened, as you'll recall, over the 12's. Where a 20 can give adequate pattern density for quail when bored improved cylinder, the 28 may have to be tightened to modified to approximate the pattern density of the bigger gauge. Naturally, this makes it a trifle harder to hit with.

But for a real sporty gauge—one that is capable of taking most of our small, short-range upland birds, and doing it with authority—the 28 is hard to beat. But remember: the 28 has to be used at short ranges!

The .410 Bore

The .410 is a fun target gun, and probably fun for shooting pigeons out of the barn loft. But for most people, it has no place in the uplands. It is a crippler with pitiful patterns, woeful shot stringing, and not enough shot to do anything past twenty-five yards.

It is not a kid's gun, but an expert's gun, and there aren't enough experts around to make it worthwhile. If it weren't used in skeet competition, the bore—not a true gauge—would probably be dead by now. I don't like the .410, as you've probably guessed, because it is a crippler and a maimer and not a killer; our birds deserve better than that. Sorry if you feel otherwise. End of discussion.

The 16-Gauge

The 16 is, they say, about to die a slow, painful death. They say the ammunition is going out of production. They say that there is no reason for the gauge to exist. They say that almost no one uses it anymore. Baloney and phooey.

The 16 was once the gentleman's gauge, the unavoidable choice for the experienced birdshooter who gunned partridge in the Northeast or quail in the Deep South. This man considered the 12 for ducks and geese, and the 20 as a trainer for his sons or wife. A bird hunter carried a 16.

Once the 16 was a good compromise because it had some of the authority of a 12 while it had some of the lines and feel of a 20—the best of both worlds. Then, gun companies, seeking to maximize profits, started putting 16-gauge barrels on 12-gauge frames, and suddenly the 16 had the weight and feel of a 12. And, as load offerings were expanded for the 20 and decreased for the 16, suddenly the typical 16-gauge offered the *worst* of both worlds—inadequate load-ings coupled with increased weight. If you want light and fast, go with the 20; if you want range and power, pack a 12.

It worked out that way, and the sales of 16-gauge guns around the world and 16-gauge shells in this country have continued to decline. But I think there's a renaissance of sorts going on among some shoot-ers. The 16-gauge shooter is a traditionalist. He knows the gauge's past glory, and he wants a little of that Americana in his gun cabinet and in his coverts.

The 16-gauge fan has also discovered the used gun market, and it's crawling with good 16-gauges at prices lower than those com-manded by the 20s and 12s. I had an L. C. Smith featherweight 16 that cost me half what a comparable 20 would have cost. A plain Field Grade, it still has the classic sidelock lines I like so well. I'm sorry I sold it.

My brush gun is a 16-gauge Parker, another low-grade gun, but with it in the grouse and woodcock coverts, I feel like a sport, and it performs well for me. My one and only really good British game gun is a 16, too. This one weighs but five-and-a-half pounds.

What these have in common is the fact that they were all built back when the 16 had the weight of a modern 20 with nearly the power of a 12—the best-of-both-worlds time in American gun-making history.

In the South, the 16 is still used fairly extensively, but it is used primarily by older gunners who have been using their old standbys for decades. When these men walk in on their last covey, the 16's popularity will probably diminish further.

The 16-gauge was developed with one ounce of shot in mind, and it is this load that it shoots efficiently—perhaps more efficiently than any other gauge, and virtually all of them will or can be made to shoot one ounce—the 28 now being a handload proposition for one ounce of shot. But, time and again, we see that one ounce is all that's needed for a lot of upland hunting situations. The one-and-one-eighth-ounce loads currently available for the 16 are, to my way of thinking, a bit too much, although when pushed by two-and-three-quarter drams of powder, this amount of shot in #6 is a nice little pheasant load if the ranges are not extreme—say, inside thirty yards.

Still, the romance and tradition remains with those who carry 16-gauge guns into the coverts. The gun, like so many of those who carry it, is a throwback to another time and place in this country, a time we'd like to go back to, if even for a little while.

Gun Weight

Outside of what makes a good-looking woman, I don't think any subject is more open to debate than what constitutes proper gun weight.

For example, my pal Gene Hill likes guns to have some substance to them, preferring guns that run toward seven pounds. Hill says that anything lighter is tough to swing and leads to stopping the gun, and you end up missing.

But Hilly is a big man—biceps like a Tartar, and his hands are like those of a baseball catcher, which he was. To him, a seven-pound gun is a wand. On the other hand, I'm a little guy—about five feet ten inches, and I don't weigh one fifty with my pockets full of traploads. To me, seven pounds is a lot of gun.

There are quite a few old chestnuts about gun weight, like: "A heavier gun keeps the swing going; once you get it started, it's hard to stop." (What they don't say is: "But it's also damned hard to get it going!") Or: "A heavier gun soaks up recoil." True, but a lot of people don't shoot enough ever to have recoil become a factor. Most of that recoil business comes from target shooters, who pop tens of thousands of primers a year, not from the three-box-a-season game shooter. When the feathers and adrenalin are up, most of us don't feel the kick.

The matter of gun weight in itself is a sort of history lesson in gunmaking. Years ago, when the United States was mostly wilderness, a gun was made to last, with little attention to the niceties that Europe had become accustomed to. Americans traveled far and wide and had little time to send their guns off to a smith for repair should something break, and the closest such craftsman could well be a couple of territories away.

To counter this problem in the days before high-grade steels and modern metallurgy (which came about between the World Wars), parts were "overmade"; that is, they were made large and, of necessity, heavy to ensure reliability. The tradition has sort of stuck, aided by our affinity for large shot loads, which require a gun that won't come apart after a case of shells.

Additionally, because there is no official proof house in the U. S., guns continue to be made a bit heavier so that the shooter doesn't have the thing blow up in his face. With an official proof house, as exists in nearly all of the European gunmaking countries, it is possible to have a gun tested according to standards set by a government, and then certified by that government. This moves the liability from the maker to the government should something be amiss with a gun—and we all know how fighting city hall comes out.

Without such a proof house here, the liability continues to be on the heads of the makers, thus—even with modern steels and heat-treating of parts—our manufacturers are hesitant to bring the weights of shotguns down to what Europeans have found comfortable—and to what they should be for the proper dynamics inherent in a fine game gun.

Proper weight is also dependent in large part upon the game being hunted. A seven-pound dove gun with long barrels won't do the job in the woodcock coverts. The dove gun is carried little and—we hope—shot a lot. So for most people, the seven-pound gun swings smoothly and follows through better at these targets in the open.

However, in places where shots are short and fast, a gun that comes in at around six pounds is better for most people. This gun is carried a lot and shot little, and the shots taken are fast and of the snap variety. Still, speed is dependent on balance; a well-balanced gun of seven pounds will be faster in the hands than a poorly balanced gun of a pound less in weight.

So discussing gun weight is really discussing balance *and* weight together—I don't see how you can separate them.

For brush shooting (ruffed grouse, woodcock, quail in thickets, and so forth), I've found that a gun with the weight toward the rear handles faster and comes up quicker. But such a gun is hard to learn to use well because it is so unforgiving. You have to provide all of the momentum for the follow-through, and you are the one that can easily stop the swing. But "swing" is often a cruel word in the brush: You rarely get the chance for an official swing; more of a mount-and-poke is what normally happens. A light—under six-and-a-half pounds—gun with the muzzles decidedly light can be a deadly weapon for this type of shooting, but one that can just as easily make you miss if you aren't always aware of its shortcomings.

In the open (doves, western quail and other western birds, and prairie pheasants), the gun with the balance farther forward is a better choice. But, like the muzzle-light gun, the extremes are to be avoided. We're talking about a matter of fractions of an inch at the balance point; a muzzle-light gun balances maybe one-half to three-quarters of an inch rear of the hinge pin on a double, with the muzzle-heavy gun balancing the same distance ahead of the hinge pin.

Balance can be achieved by the addition or subtraction of weight in the gun. A gun can be made to feel lighter by adding weight to the stock—lead in the hollow of the stock under the recoil pad or butt plate. Or wood can be removed from the same area to give the weight bias to the barrels.

Barrels can be lopped off a couple of inches and screw-in chokes installed to give more barrel lightness. The gun becomes a better overall performer because of the flexibility of options that these chokes give the shooter. None of the really good shooters I know owns a gun that hasn't had something changed—fit, balance, or whatever. Tinkering with a gun is not only fun, it also gets you closer to realizing your full potential as a shooter.

It's funny, really, to be with a couple of these shooters where there are a lot of guns around. Take a gun show, for example. Every gun that is picked up and handled is discussed. Barrels can be opened, they say; stocks on those can be bent up or sanded down, they say; that gun can have some weight trimmed out of the stock to make the barrels handle smoother, they say. It just goes on and on. But people like this have learned what to do to make a gun work for them and not against them.

You often read and hear about how short barrels are faster than longer barrels, but this is more a function of the gun's balance than it is of the weight. I have a French 12-gauge that weighs a few ounces

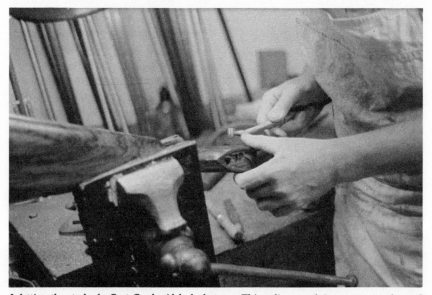

Inletting the stock of a Best Grade sidelock shotgun. This tedious work is one reason why such guns cost as much as a house did a few years ago. Here, gunmaker Nick Makinson uses a modified dentist's drill to shave off minute pieces of wood.

The inletted stock and the lock mechanism for a sidelock gun. The sidelock action, older than the boxlock, is strong in the metal workings but weaker in the wood because of the inletting necessary. Light loads are recommended. The locks are really just outside hammers whose shape has been changed to allow them to be placed as they are. Easily removed for cleaning, the locks on this gun will outlive the owner's great-grandchildren.

over five-and-a-half pounds, and its twenty-seven-and-a-half-inch barrels are very fast because the balance is correct for this weight and gauge. It is a two-and-a-half-inch gun — chambered for shells that length. I shoot these short shells, which are becoming more and more available here. Because of its age, I dare not have the chambers lengthened for two-and-three-quarter-inch American shells with their higher chamber pressures.

However, I recently got a nice boxlock English Best Grade game gun, circa 1920, which was a two-and-a-half-inch gun. Before I brought it into this country, I had the Englishman I bought it from get the chambers lengthened to two-and-three-quarter inches and then send it off to the London proof house to be reproved with nitro loads. It came through fine. By the way, this is the law there: Any tampering with the metal of a shotgun, and it has to go to proof again. We don't have that law here — no official proof house in the U. S. of A.

I guess what I'm saying is that most of us tamper and tinker with our guns, or otherwise bedevil a perfectly harmless gunsmith to get a gun that's fit for what we want. But that's not even half of the fight; the other part is using the thing the right way.

The hand-rubbed oil finish is a craft unto itself. Most good stockmakers have a secret formula, but the main ingredient to a fine finish is grease from the stockmaker's elbows.

Stock Fitting

Getting a custom stock fitted, or getting one altered so that it does fit, is the basis on which a custom gun rests. The stock is the sighting mechanism of a shotgun, because the rear sight is the eye, in effect. If the rear sight is raised, as with a rifle's elevation on its rear sight, the front sight—in this case the muzzles—has to be raised to stay in line, and the shot charge goes high. Everything is vice versa if the stock is too low.

The high and low of a stock refer to the comb, the part of the stock against which the cheek rests. The angle that the stock slopes on top from the front to the back (heel) is the determinant of whether the stock is crooked or not. A crooked stock starts with a comb measurement that is substantially higher than the heel measurement, and anything more than a one-and-a-half-inch disparity between these two is considered crooked.

A crooked stock has a place, oddly enough. I've found that fast brush shooting is done with a little more ease with a crooked stock—one with a high comb and a low heel. My pet brush gun has a comb drop from the line of the rib of one-and-a-quarter inches—very high—and a heel drop of two-and-five-eighths inches—quite low. I seem to

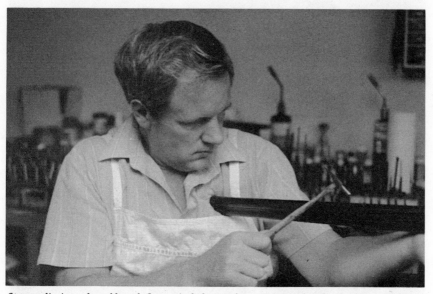

Stress-relieving a dented barrel. Successively larger plugs are inserted under the dent, and a brass hammer is used to bring the dent up gradually to the level of the surrounding metal without weakening the tube.

Joining the action and barrel assembly of a handmade gun. Good gunmakers use lampblack to detect minute spots where friction can cause problems.

shoulder this stock quickly with little or no ducking to the stock to compensate. Does it kick (one of the criticisms of crooked stocks)? Yep—but I don't shoot that many shots in a day with it, so I don't notice it that much.

The straight, high stock is grand for birds such as pheasants that have a normally high-flushing tendency. The target is climbing, and a gun that, in effect, shoots *up* at the mark compensates for some of this. A high stock also goes a long way toward conquering head-lifting, because you can see nicely with your face down on the stock, making it unnecessary to lift your face to see what's happening out there.

The length of the stock should be enough so that you don't bang your nose with your hand during recoil, yet short enough so that the gun won't get tangled during mounting. Most of us could shoot longer stocks better, the mounting entanglements being a function of no practice. A long stock makes you pull the stock into your face, making head-lifting more difficult—but not impossible.

A stock can be cut off if it's too long—maintaining the proper angle of pitch—or a recoil pad added if it's too short. For the comb-heel changes, a stock that's too high or straight can be worked down and refinished, but the too-low stock is a toughie. There are a number

Barrels being readied for brazing together. One of the hardest tasks a double-gun maker faces is getting the barrels joined and then regulated to shoot to the same point of aim at forty yards.

of good stock people who do bending work: The stock, after being treated at the grip in a hot oil bath, becomes pliable enough for a bender's jig—or his thigh—to bend the stock upward. If the bend is drastic, a new angle may have to be cut for the pitch of the stock, the angle at which the butt is cut off. Then the stock is dried, perhaps refinished, and you have a custom stock out of an old one. This procedure isn't cheap, but it's preferable to getting a new stock made, given the price of good walnut; it also allows you to keep intact the original wood and inletting on a fine old gun.

Let's say that you can't live without a custom stock, one built for you from the butt forward, and your lifelong dream is to get fitted for a piece of wood to go on your own custom gun. Or let's say that you are going to place an order for one of the fine European guns that offer the custom-stock option at no increased cost, but that you have to know your measurements before you can place the order.

Both of these options require you to get fitted if you are fuzzy about your dimensions. There are places that do this—the Orvis Shooting Schools, for instance—and many gun companies that deal with custom stocks have people available for gun fitting—AYA, of Spain, has gun fitters in this country, representatives who do the measuring prior to the placing of an order.

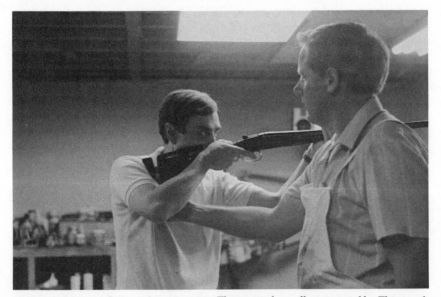

Author undergoes a fitting using a try gun. These guns have all parts movable. They can be adjusted for length of pull, drop at comb and heel, pitch, and cast off/on.

For the owner of a 12-gauge game gun who wants to make sure his molars stay intact when he shoots, a couple of light but very effective loads. The British shells are two-and-a-half inches long, making them suitable for short-chambered European guns.

They all rely upon the use of a try gun for their fitting, no matter who they are. The try gun is a regular shotgun, normally a side-by-side double, that has all the salient parts of the stock capable of being adjusted mechanically. The comb can be raised or lowered, the butt extended to increase the length of pull (distance from the trigger to the center of the butt), the pitch can be changed up, down, or neutral, the cast-off can be adjusted, and so forth.

Most Americans are only vaguely familiar with "cast-off" and its opposite, "cast-on." Cast is the degree that the stock of a shotgun bends from the shooter's face. On almost all shotguns made for the U. S. market, there is no cast. You can look down the length of a shotgun from the rear of the stock and see a straight line down the rib and down the top of the stock.

With cast-off, the stock is slanted away from the face of a right-handed shooter. (Cast-on sees the stock slanted toward the face of a right-handed shooter; left-handers shoot stocks with cast-on—which for them is cast-off.) Cast-off exists because the British, and some others, are convinced that the cast will bring the rib in line with the eye more easily. However, most Americans simply place their heads over the top of the stock, turn their faces slightly, and achieve the same effect. Lots of people argue with me about this, but I think we shoot just fine with stocks that are dead neutral because of the way we've learned to mount guns. Yes, fellow Yanks, we mount guns wrong and we shoot castless stocks, which are also wrong, yet we do a good job of holding our own in the game fields around the world, don't we?

Now, the fitting process is not idiot-proof. Fitters, like those who more closely resemble human beings, have their own biases. The best fitter for the game shooter is the one who fits for that sport. An English fitter who fits stocks mostly for driven-bird shooting does less well on guns intended for our style of walk-up shooting. Trap and skeet stocks are another story, as are guns intended for competitive live-pigeon shooting. There are specialists for those sports.

The experienced fitter will ask you questions, such as what type of clothing you'll be wearing (the thickness will affect the fit of the stock), the type of cover you'll be hunting in, and so forth. All of these things make his job more complicated, so a well-fit, all-around stock really doesn't do the trick. I've made the point that not only guns and loads change with the game for success, but the fit of a stock could be slightly different depending upon the game to be hunted. A gun for pheasant shooting, for example, should be higher shooting than one intended for quail. This means a slight variation in gun fit—at least to me.

Some people are hard to fit. I'm one, because I'm so bloody chicken-necked that I need a stock a full two inches longer than the normal person of my height and arm length. Problem is, I just don't shoot well with a gun that long in the stock. Fitters tell me that with practice I'll do well with a long stock. I tell 'em to drop over someplace hot, and I'll shoot my shorter stocks and be happy.

Anyhow, using the try gun, the fitter gets the measurements close so that he's pretty sure the gun is pointing about where you're looking. Then off you go to get the fine-tuning down pat. This means shooting, and stay away from any fitter who pronounces your measurements perfect without some test firing using the try gun.

This firing is done, normally, at whitewashed steel plates that show where patterns impact and that are then painted over for another, immediate, try. At the staid old English gun houses, you'll be trundled from downtown to the shooting grounds for this final session.

As you fire, minor adjustments are made in the try gun until the patterns are being placed where you're looking. Then, there is usually a go at some moving targets such as clays. Many times, the fit that

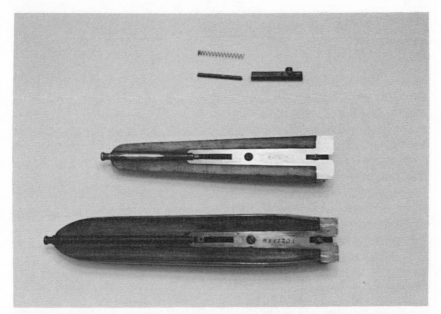

Two forends for the same gun. The forend above has had both its metal and wood scaled down to a splinter for speed of handling and for a more traditional look. Note the number of parts that have been removed to effect the change.

works on a stationary target doesn't work on a moving target, because perhaps the fitee, for example, cheeks his stock more deeply shooting at the pattern plate than he ever will when the mark is flying. (Most of us do just that, by the way.)

When the stock is performing correctly for the shooter, the measurements are recorded and you're all set either to have the stock made there or to take the measurements with you for a stock you plan to have built later.

I think that the best fit is the one the shooter works out for himself, provided he's thoughtful about the whole thing and gives his experience and his needs a chance to tell him something.

For example, let's say that Our Hero constantly shoots his rising pheasants too far back, failing to get pattern placement into the head–neck area. This could indicate that the gun is shooting too low, and the stock's drop should be decreased in one of the ways mentioned earlier.

Or let's say that a brush-country quail hunter is shooting over the top of low single birds, and he's doing it with a regularity that's frightening. He may want to take the comb down a bit. This is what I

The point of impact can be raised by heightening the comb of a shotgun, the gun's "rear sight."
One option is having the stock bent by a gunsmith who first softens the wood with hot oil. The
other option, shown here, is to place a comb pad on the stock, using Velcro strips. This is a fine
alternative, because sometimes a gun should shoot higher than at other times, and the pad can be
removed or put back any number of times.

The proof of the fit is in the shooting. Here, Bryan Bilinski, a qualified fitter, checks the
adjustments on a try gun for a client.

Bilinski watches as the shooter mounts and fires at a steel, whitewashed plate. At this stage, the shooter is told to mount and fire quickly, without dwelling on the gun but instead concentrating on the target.

mean by letting your experience work for you. The perfect arrangement is to let a fitter get you close, and then let your experience take over from there for the final fitting.

The configuration of the wood parts of a shotgun is various, but standard. The classic form calls for a straight grip—sometimes called the "English style"—and a small splinter-type forend. For years this has been the standard on guns coming from Britain and most of continental Europe. This style kinks the triggering hand somewhat, causing the elbow to rise, thus making it more difficult to raise the head during the pointing process—at least that's how it seems to work for me.

The small splinter forend normally serves two functions: to house the ejector mechanism and to hold the barrels to the action body. The extractors, on guns with no ejectors, are activated here as well. The off hand grips the barrels on a double—the side-by-side, anyway—rather than the forend.

The straight grip stock comes into action more quickly, many shooters feel, and additionally makes head-lifting more difficult. But when coupled with the splinter forend, this style brings the hands onto the same plane and very close to the plane on which the barrels are shooting. In other words, the shot charge seems to go *through the hands* to the mark.

The straight grip can be used on a repeating gun as well, and makes for a nicer-pointing gun. Remington currently makes an autoloader with a straight grip, and Ithaca makes a very lightweight pump so stocked; they handle well and look nice. A gunsmith can grind off the grip of a regular stock on a repeater and rechecker the new straight grip for you. If you haven't shot this style, it takes a little getting used to, but you'll end up doing better once it's mastered. An English-stocked, sidelock shotgun is the most beautiful firearm in the world.

Most repeating guns have the more generally seen pistol grip, and many doubles do as well. Over/unders are made with small forends and straight grips, but more are made with larger forends and pistol grips. Some side-by-side doubles are made with both the large, hand-filling beavertail forend and pistol grip, among them the Winchester

The view from the rear as the shot charge leaves the gun. A good fitter can see the shot charge in the air as a greyish disturbance around the target. Adjustments are made after several shots, once a pattern has been established about which way the shooter is firing. Not all fitters agree on what constitutes proper fit. Bilinski prefers a high stock with the shooter's eye substantially above the rib, as is the style voiced by Robert Churchill; others like the rib and the eye to be in closer alignment. Most modern coaches prefer the former method.

Model 21 when it was an off-the-rack item years ago. Today that gun is as much of a custom number as a Purdey, so there is no longer any norm. But any custom gun can be ordered with this beavertail–pistol grip combination.

The two work together to keep the hands on the same plane, much like the splinter forend–straight grip. The large beavertail acts with the pistol grip to bring the hands in line, but this combination finds the hands well below the line of the shot charge as it emanates from the plane of the bores, unlike the classical style, which has the hands right on that plane.

Whichever style suits you is fine, as long as you don't mix the styles, such as a beavertail with a straight grip or a splinter forend with a pistol grip (like most of the old Parker and L. C. Smith and some other guns of a bygone era). The hands will level out, and they will rise or drop to find this level. So if your gun has a splinter forend and a pistol grip, it will shoot low as the forend hand drops to meet the plane established by the grip hand.

Chokes

The concept of choke is not going to be labored here—too much. But there are some things you should understand, especially if your patterns aren't what you'd like.

First, don't ever believe the manufacturer's markings on the barrel or barrels as to choke designation. You have to shoot patterns, and the best way is to look at the patterns your gun throws at the ranges you normally shoot your game. What the gun shoots like at twenty-five yards is probably more important than what the percentages work out to at forty.

Second, you can, to a great degree, adjust the choke by using different shot sizes/brands. Hard shot patterns tighter; soft shot patterns more openly. The British two-and-a-half-inch shell is a sweet little unit because of the way it patterns—nice and even. Pattern fails before penetration, we know; in other words, the pattern goes to pieces quite a few yards short of the place that the shot loses its force to down a bird, so a good pattern is a must.

I have found in discussing this subject with friends that most of us have had the experience of using a lousy gun with lousy shells and still killing birds, that the matter of proper shooting technique and the right fit outweigh attention to pattern—if the gun is pointed right, the bird will probably come down most of the time.

If you have to make a choice between having too much choke or

Noting the pattern placement. A good pattern for upland shooting will have, in most cases, about sixty percent of the shot charge striking above the point of aim to compensate for rising birds, the most common upland-gunning situation.

too little for the job at hand, take too much; you can always wait for them to get out there a bit more before you fire should the birds come up underfoot.

And don't forget that all things change with time. Just as a gun that fit us when we were forty-five may not at seventy-five, so the need for pattern changes.

Where once a loose improved cylinder may have been perfect open-country quail choking, now we may have to go to a modified. Many people cross this off to reaction time slowing with age, but reaction times seem to be constant through adulthood. What changes is our intensity—maybe it doesn't seem as important to get this bird this time, so we slow a bit. Perhaps our hearing, the first of the senses we use to locate flushing birds, has dulled with time so that we hear the birds after they are up and partially away instead of just as they clatter from the grass.

These things dictate tighter chokes; the man who is training a dog or a boy needs tighter chokes as well. The dog trainer before he fires wants to make sure the dog is steady; the boy trainer before he shoots wants to make sure the young man gets a shot. Both of these situations require that the bird will be out there before our turn comes, if it comes at all: tighter chokes again.

Switching from a cheap target load to a high-quality pigeon load will tighten patterns about one degree—say, from modified to full. Remember, most of the "game loads" sold at attractive prices are real cheapos made with little antimony and shot that, charitably, could be a bit rounder.

If more pattern is needed, a gunsmith can take out some metal from the choke area of the barrels, and some can install screw-in chokes, a dandy answer. Or shooting the cheap shot can spread the pattern. But remember: Those shot in the widest portion of the spread are deformed ones affected by air pressure, and thus they are slower and have less penetration compared to the shot in the center portion of the pattern. So if you choose this route, keep the ranges very short. For example, I shoot very cheap shells at woodcock, good ones at pheasants. By the way, you will not go broke buying shotgun shells— you go broke buying shotguns and trips to exotic places to use them. I know!

The Game Gun Concept

Imagine yourself in this scene: The drizzle is falling lightly on you and your shooting companions, fanned out as you are along the firing line. Dressed in your tweeds with a waterproof jacket to turn the chill, you stamp your feet, part in anticipation, part because of the November cold.

Ahead of you, in the forest, the beaters are just starting their drive. Quietly they move along, slowly pushing the pheasants into the air, now, a few at a time, lest the drive be over too quickly with too many lost shooting opportunities that large flocks are heir to.

Many times this day, you'll shoot at high pheasants, birds born and reared here for you and the other guests. The gun you carry is the traditional game gun—the pinnacle of shotgunning art blended with science and function.

As American shooters become more compatible with English thinking, the game gun has taken on new stature here on this continent. As shooting becomes less a matter of putting meat on the table and more an experience, it is natural that the game gun should find its way into the hearts and gun cabinets of Americans.

Let's take a look at the game gun.

The game gun is, essentially, a double shotgun, a side-by-side, made very light and intended to shoot relatively light loads. The gun may be made for driven-bird shooting, or for walk-up shooting like we do here in this part of the world.

These guns are also works of art in terms of fit, finish, engraving, color casehardening, and wood pattern. Almost universally, game guns feature straight grips and splinter forends, and although the sidelock style is most often seen, the boxlock also qualifies.

One thing that they all have in common is durability. Some game guns have been fired in excess of a million times at shooting schools in England, and they're still going strong. This is because only the best steels are used, and those steels are properly heat-treated to provide the elasticity and the strength needed to stand up to the pounding of thousands of shells. But, with proper care, virtually any well-made firearm will do the same thing these days. Modern metallurgy has all but eliminated the problem of guns working loose, if they're of good manufacture, so spending thousands to ensure reliability just doesn't make much sense these days.

The game gun is a custom item, with the owners being fitted for a custom stock usually by a little gnome of a stockfitter in a poorly lit back room somewhere. These people know what they're doing, and the result is usually pleasing.

Game guns are made, as I've said, to be used with light loads. The British have long settled on the 12-gauge as the bore of choice, and the shot loads are regulated to the game—from as little as seven-eighths of an ounce to one-and-a-quarter ounces for waterfowl. But the standard game load is a one-and-one-sixteenth-ounce load for a 12-gauge in a two-and-a-half-inch shell. This load is effective on driven game where the speed of the incoming bird and the speed of the outgoing shot charge make for a dandy and deadly collision up there twenty-five to thirty-five yards. Additionally, the incoming game has its vitals exposed more than the outgoing targets we normally fire at here.

The balance on a game gun is between the hands—at the hinge pin, specifically. This way, the gun spins on this fulcrum and handles fast. But weight bias can be built in for the muzzles or the stock, depending upon choice and use. Overall, their lightness is what first grabs the newcomer's attention. A 12-gauge gun weighs about what an American-made 20 will weigh—right around six-and-a-half pounds, and most often it has twenty-seven-and-a-half- or twenty-eight-and-a-half-inch barrels, although twenty-six- and—especially—twenty-five-inch barrels are common.

Game guns are often delivered with the oak-and-leather case and the other accoutrements I discuss in another section [see "Gear"], and these touches don't come free, either. In all, ordering a game gun these days is a matter of considerable financial outlay. For example, as this is being written, a Purdey shotgun, probably the best known and perhaps the most prestigious, sells for in excess of $20,000 – and probably closer to $25,000. And the gun takes several years to be completed for delivery.

Contrary to popular belief, however, the British don't tell you what you ought to have, they allow the customer to tell them. If you want a rib that is substantially different than what they suggest, they may look at you funny, but they'll make it for you; the customer's always right.

Mechanically, the game gun always comes with selective ejectors, but single and double triggers are a matter of choice, with two triggers still the most common. Some are self-opening or at least assisted-opening guns, with a large spring that helps the shooter drop the barrels quickly in the heat of combat on the firing line. These guns close hard, too, as the spring gets reset for the next opening. It's a little hard to get used to.

Among the over-and-unders, a number qualify as game guns for the same reasons I've listed previously: workmanship, weight, fit, finish, and balance. But the side-by-side remains the really traditional gun.

Some game guns come with interchangeable barrels to mate with the same action; others come in matched pairs with different chokes but identical otherwise.

Now, customizing a gun so that you have something of a game gun facsimile is not difficult, but among those in the know, it will never qualify as the real thing. Still, a good double can be fitted, a new stock made or an old one bent, and you have a gun that is almost – but not quite – made for you. Still, in the field, it makes little difference to the bird. But then, it does to us.

That's why, eventually, a lot of us crazies either dream about buying or actually do buy a real game gun by a British maker. Used, one can be had for pennies on the dollar for what the same gun would sell for today new, yet it retains its value, even appreciates in value as the years roll by. Some of the older guns, in my opinion, are better than the new game guns being turned out. A British gun made after WWI and before WWII is going to last forever, make you proud, and it won't cost what a new one does.

There are some inherent dangers present in buying an older gun. If you pick up one made in continental Europe or England, there is a better than even chance that the gun is one that's chambered for the short, two-and-a-half-inch shell, the standard case size in many foreign countries.

This seems to be more common among guns that are smaller than 12-gauge, although it happens among this bigger bore as well. Most guns made for the American market—all guns, nowadays, really—are chambered for the longer two-and-three-quarter-inch American case, some even three-inch, if the gun was made as a waterfowl piece.

If you fire standard (American) shells in a short-chambered gun, you are in for a thrill. The gun will kick like a .458 Winchester, the patterns will be blown, and you could very likely cause irreparable harm to your gun and to yourself. The standard shell chambers easily because the two-and-three-quarter-inch shell fits. But when it's fired, the crimp cannot open fully in the chamber, placing tremendous pressure on the forcing cone just forward of the chamber. Such guns crack like rifles.

If you are buying an older gun, check the barrel flats for markings. These may appear as the numeral 65, indicating that the chamber is sixty-five millimeters long—about two-and-a-half inches.

Your options then consist of having the chambers lengthened (and reproofed, if you are buying the gun in Europe for import into the States) or shooting the shorter shells. Since the balance, weight, and design of a two-and-a-half-inch gun are slightly different than guns chambered for two-and-three-quarter inches, I prefer the latter course. The shells are getting easier to come by, and they pattern well. Yes, they're made in waterproof plastic. These shells are nice even in guns with standard, for us, chambers. Although some folks say differently, I've never noticed any difference in the patterns thrown by a short shell in a longer chamber.

Buying an Old Gun

If it hasn't started already, I'm going to predict that over the next decade or two, you're going to see a lot of fine old guns by really good foreign and domestic gunmakers actually being used in the coverts to shoot at birds.

Part of the reason for this is the natural evolution that hunters have been going through: the seeking of a total experience. With very few of us having an opportunity to take a limit of birds every time out and many of us not taking a limit through choice, good dog work, a day away from work, and the pleasures of the uplands are enough—thankfully.

Such names as Parker, L. C. Smith, Purdey, Boss, Webley & Scott, and others are starting to take their places with this generation of upland hunters. (The old American classics are a trip back in time all by themselves.) They provide the thrill of owning, carrying, and shooting a light gun, and also fit American hunters' increasingly British outlook (check the mail-order catalogs once if you disbelieve). And so there is no longer going to be the affinity toward the 20-bore as *the* upland gun like there has been of late; light 12s and 16s that come in at or around six-and-a-half pounds make dandy shotguns for our needs, and the better names all are balanced far better than something you can buy off the rack in the *splattermatic* persuasion.

And there's the economic factor. I recently saw a listing of fine old doubles — still shootable and by good makers — which were priced at only slightly more than you'd pay for a couple new pump guns at the hardware store.

With a relatively small initial investment, and then a few more outlays for getting things modernized a bit, you can have the gun of your dreams for a price not too much higher than you'd pay for a modern, domestic over/under or side-by-side.

The problem, then, becomes one of finding a shootable piece with the configuration you want and knowing what to do to the thing to get it just *so* once you've chosen it. (If you are a collector and want to get a gun in original condition and keep it that way, you probably won't hunt with it anyway. So set aside the worry of altering and ruining a collector's item.)

Let's say you migrate through Uncle Friendly's Gun Shop one fine day and there before you is a rack of good guns. You start checking.

The first thing you'll notice is that the 20-gauges are priced uniformly higher than 12s, and 16s are the cheapest yet. But once you start hefting and feeling, you'll notice that all of them handle about the same — such is the case with fine guns. In truth, the better side-by-sides of foreign ancestry are lighter in 12-bore than most of our domestic, modern 20s. If the weight is right, don't be a snob about gauge. And forget the crap about finding shells for a 16 — all three of the major ammunition companies have a good line of shells for this gauge with no plans to drop production.

So you start looking, hefting them one at a time. Let's say you set aside several to be looked at more closely. The first thing to do is check the wear factor. The opening lever on a double moves farther to the left as it wears. If a double has the lever in the far-left position when the gun is closed, put it back in the rack and go on.

If the lever is not too far left (less than one-eighth inch) or is straight back, there has been little wear. Open this gun and, grasping the grip in one hand and the forend in the other, twist gently back and forth in a side-to-side motion. A gun that's "loose" will rattle like castanets when you do this; a tight one won't. If you aren't sure, remove the forend, partially open the gun, and try again.

Then, take a hair from your head (or someone else's), place it so that half of it is down by a firing pin hole and the other half sticking up, and close the gun. In a tight gun, the hair will be caught in the breech; if it's not, the gun may be too loose. So if it catches, you're okay.

Next, look down the barrels as you point them at a strong light. Look for holes, marks where the barrels could have been bent at one time, or huge scars left from pitting. If there's nothing monumental, call Uncle Friendly over and have him measure the chambers for you. Many early American and foreign guns, as I mentioned earlier, had chambers shorter than two-and-three-quarter inches. If you've got a short-chambered gun, you can have the chambers lengthened, or get some of the two-and-a-half-inch foreign shells.

Now, check the firing mechanism. A pair of fired shells in the gauge you're handling, or "snap caps" (dummy cartridges), will allow you to check the trigger pull safely. The hammers should let off crisply and lightly. If you're testing a double-trigger shotgun, remember that the Continentals and English have the rear trigger (left barrel) set to go off with a slightly harder pull, to prevent accidental discharge of that barrel. So don't be alarmed if the triggers don't pull evenly; on fine guns, they probably won't. Really excessive difference is not good, though.

Once the triggers have been pulled, open the gun to check how well the ejectors work (or extractors, if the gun has those instead). The ejectors should throw the shells well away and both the same distance. Reload with your snap caps and repeat one barrel at a time to make sure the ejectors work well, independently for each barrel.

Next, after you've satisfied yourself that the gun operates, check for any cracks in the metal—a 10x hand lens helps here—but there probably won't be any, so move on to the wood. Remove the forend and check for cracks where the forend iron is inletted into the wood. Check the grip for cracks. These generally result when someone starts shooting heavy loads through a light double. If you're planning to have the gun custom stocked, you can forget this part of it, but if the stock measurements are good enough for you to shoot as is or with minor alterations, look the wood over thoroughly.

Disregard the finish on the wood—you can always have another finish applied, or do it yourself. Same with the checkering—a good wood man can cut you a new pattern or deepen the existing one for a few dollars. These are things that can be made right again cheaply.

Naturally, you wouldn't be messing with a gun with Damascus or "twist" barrels. If you don't know if you have such a gun or not, look at the barrels under the forend. If there's a definite swirl pattern in the metal, these are soft iron and shouldn't be fired as is. But with a certain procedure, they *can* be fired. Here's how: Several places in the United States will cut the barrels off forward of the chamber and then insert modern steel tubes in place of the old barrels full length right through the old chambers. A 12- or 16-bore can even be "sleeved down" to 20-gauge this way, and new chokes bored in. This is expensive, though. My suggestion is to stay away from soft-iron barrels unless you want a wall hanger.

Next, and this takes some doing, you want to take the gun out of the shop to have an independent gunsmith check things out. I'd suggest that you write Uncle Friendly a check for the full price and ask him to hold it for twenty-four hours while you have the gun looked at. Tell him you want an agreement that allows you to return the gun and get your check back in that time if you decide against the gun. If he's reputable, he'll have little problem with this, although he may want the check replaced with a charge-card imprint first so he doesn't get stiffed.

Take the gun to a gunsmith and have him strip it down to look it over. Get prices on new wood (if needed), reblueing (if you want), recut checkering, and a new hinge pin if your newfound jewel is a little loose. Add these to the purchase price, and you've got an idea of what the thing will cost you under the bottom line.

If you decide this is *the* shotgun, go back to Unc's place and dicker. Normally, used guns have the same percentage of built-in money to play with as do used cars. Make an offer. At the most, you'll still have to pay only the stated asking price. Your sales acumen figures in here, but I'd suggest not crawling up to the gunshop proprietor on your knees and salivating if you expect a very good deal.

At this point, try to get an agreement with him—in writing—that if anything major turns up wrong with the gun in the next thirty to sixty days, you can bring it back. He may balk at this a little, but assure him you wouldn't hold him responsible for something *you* do to the gun once it leaves the shop. With some fine shotguns, "letters of authenticity" are available. These tell something of the history of the gun. Ask for them, but if they *are* available, they would have probably been produced already.

In most cases, the best guns are going to be found through specialty gun dealers who deal with these items, places like William Larkin Moore, Pachmyar, and others. Then, your deal has to be consummated by mail or phone. Such places will usually ask you to send a certified check for the gun in advance, but they allow anywhere from three to five days for you to inspect the gun. After that time, it must be returned or the sale is considered final.

The guns sold in this manner are usually shipped via United Parcel Service to a registered holder of a Federal Firearms License (FFL). It is your responsibility to obtain a copy of a valid FFL, have the dealer sign it, and send it to the shipper. The gun will then be transported by UPS to the dealer where you arrange for pickup and for filling out the required federal and state forms that testify you aren't a wacko.

By the way, talking about shipping a gun, you do not need to have an FFL form if you are shipping a gun to a dealer for repair, which also means alteration such as stock work or barrel work. But to return the gun to you, the gunsmith needs the FFL from someone who has agreed to take delivery for you. If it's your local gun store, expect to pay the dealer a few bucks for his time.

Now, the gun is yours, you're basically sure it's sound, and you've already figured out a way to hide the purchase from your wife. Now is the time to go to work on it. If the stock fits you, and it may do so very well as is, fine. Get it recheckered and refinished and take it hunting.

However, a new stock job is another matter. Good shotgun stockmakers are few and far between, especially one who can fit a stock to you. If you know your measurements, say from a gun that you have that you *know* fits you, take these to a stock man and have him order up the wood. While you're waiting for the wood to come in, you can get the metal surfaces reblued if you like—this doesn't take long. Also, now is the time to shoot some patterns with the gun. If the gun doesn't shoot true to point of aim, take it back and get your money back, per the agreement. If it does but the chokes are too tight, a good barrel man can give you the borings you want by grinding a little out of the ends of the barrels, shooting the gun, grinding, shooting, etc., until the right patterns are reached. Be sure to specify what load you'll be shooting in which barrel so the testing can be done with that load.

I've seen some dandy chokes for quail, grouse, and woodcock made from guns with twenty-eight-inch modified/full barrels (too tight) by having the chokes miked and then cutting the barrels back an inch or an inch and a half so that some choke is retained in each barrel. An M/F combination can be cut back to IC/M in this manner, but if the chokes have ever been regulated at the muzzle, the gun may not shoot true. After cutting, the chokes can be re-regulated (if that's a word) to shoot to point of aim.

Since you're working on the chokes anyway, now may be the time to try one of the more esoteric but useful boring combinations, such as IC/full or cylinder/modified, putting two choke gradients between the barrels instead of the traditional one. Many fine old guns were choked with the same amount of constriction in each barrel, such as IC/IC or F/F. These lend themselves to such manipulation. But remember: It's easier to take choke *out* than put it *in*—loosening is easier than tightening. True, some choke can be put in through "jug" choking, but only about one degree (say from cylinder to IC), usually no more.

You may want to experiment with various loads to get the right choke. Hard shot, like that found in #7½ pigeon loads, makes a gun shoot tighter, and since most of these fine guns were made before the advent of shot cups and protective collars, they'll likely shoot tighter with modern loads.

Conversely, skeet loads usually spread pretty well, as do cheap field loads. If you buy a light 12-bore, the Winchester AA "Special Skeet" load is a sweetheart: light recoil, one ounce of shot, soft shot, and a short collar that lets some shot deform against the side of the barrel and thus spread even more.

If you want to go all the way in the British manner and have a light 12-bore with short chambers, try getting some of the two-and-a-half-inch game shells in #6 (which is really an American #7, an effective load no longer made in this country). These cute little shells work just great in a light 12, making such a gun, in effect, an overbored 20, because the shells hold about an ounce of shot.

To sum up, let me offer a few general words: 1) Make sure the gun is safe and that you have return rights if something originally undetected turns up. 2) Take the time to plan the stock, chokes, and loads. 3) Try for the best price possible, especially if you're buying a light 12 or 16. (I once found a beautiful 12-gauge, looked it over, and when the time came for the deal, I flat out asked the owner what the bottom line was, forget the salesmanship. I got it for several hundred dollars under the ticketed price.) 4) Think of the investment and work you'll have in such a gun in terms of modern prices and guns. For the price of a few production-grade pumps, you could be shooting an early American classic or one of Europe's finest.

How Many Guns Are Enough?

How many times have you read something like, "If you were to use only one gun, it should be a thus-and-so bored this-and-that."

Well, I don't know very many people who would read this book who would own and use just one shotgun. This continent has become populated by specialists, and even in our equipment, the jack-of-all-trades has very little place, not any more.

The screw-in choke devices have made the *possibility* of one gun more appealing, but screw-in chokes only change one factor: the choking. The others, such as weight, balance, shot capacity, action, gauge, are still unaffected. As a result, most folks still would like to have and use a lot of guns.

A question I'm often asked is, "How many guns are enough?" I'm usually asked that by people who expect me to pay bills with the money I spend on shotguns; nevertheless, they've got a point.

For upland gunning, if you hunt a lot of different species of birds, you have to start from zero and work up. Our purpose is to kill birds cleanly in the air. The killing is a function of the shot load as it is propelled by the powder charge; to hit the bird in the air is a function of fit, balance, weight, and choke (which determines the spread of the load at the normal ranges that your chosen bird is taken). The choke also is a function of killing, because it determines the number of pellet hits on the bird.

If you've ever played golf, you know that you wouldn't play a round of this insipid, stupid, maddening game (I've played) with one club. Each is meant for a specific type of shot to be played at a certain distance – the one-wood for distance and roll off the tee, the pitching wedge to drop the ball down on the green with little movement after it lands, and everything in between.

So it is with shotguns. The gun that performs flawlessly in the grouse thickets of the East is going to be at a disadvantage for shooting Hungarian partridge in the stubble of the West.

So, if you are striving to be the complete upland game shooter, your battery should contain at least these two guns, and I want you to spend the mortgage money until you've got them.

Plains Gun

This should be fairly long of barrel, about twenty-eight inches, and have its weight centered ahead of the normal balance point – say four-and-a-half inches ahead of the trigger (front trigger, on a double equipped with double triggers). This gun should be capable of handling a hefty shot charge, because often it will be used for such birds as pheasants, which require it. Because of this, it will be built sturdily – spell that h-e-a-v-y – but not overly so, because the distances we walk are long, too.

The plains gun should be stocked so that it is shooting a bit above point of aim or even slightly higher, especially if pheasants are the primary target. The high-shooting gun gives some advantage of being able to see the rising target.

I'd say that a 12-gauge of six-and-three-quarter to seven pounds would make a good plains gun for everything from pheasants to Huns. This gauge offers the greatest versatility in terms of shells available, for one thing—and that may be reason enough. The ranges most days in the wide open dictate the 12s authority.

I think I'd like screw-in chokes, too. These add little to the gun's weight, and they are handy for quickly switching if, say, you're out after long-flushing Huns and run across a bunch of quail that will hold. Then a quick change to open chokes takes little time and makes lots of sense.

The over/under may be a good choice for most people. The single sighting plane of the O/U seems at its best against an uncluttered sky, and precision is often needed with extreme-range shooting.

Brush Gun

This one is for close, short-range shooting where anything from a 28-gauge (within reason) on up will kill effectively. The short range means open chokes—improved cylinder should be the tightest you use.

The gun should be lighter than the plains gun because its close ranges require no large shot-powder charges. The light gun will come up a bit faster, maybe, at the end of the day, but this is often over-emphasized. Instead, balance is more important for speed.

Where the plains gun balances ahead of the hinge pin and four-and-a-half inches ahead of the front trigger, the brush gun should balance three to three-and-a-half inches ahead of the front trigger. This brings the barrels into action quickly. It won't swing smoothly, but most brush shots are not swings anyway—they are stabs and pokes and modified snap shots.

Because of the requirements of a brush gun, most of those in use are 20s, but there is no reason that a 12 or 16 can't be used, provided it meets what you want from it.

Weight? Right around six pounds, because so often we carry it one-handed while we fight brush with the other hand. A straight grip stock makes it faster coming up, I think, than a pistol grip, and there is no need for a beavertail forend unless you like them, and lots of people do.

This gun will take care of your woodcock, grouse, and thick-cover quail needs nicely. In a pinch, a little lead tape under the barrels will shift some weight forward for a smoother swing, if you find the need to use this gun in the open cover.

A checkered butt or a leather-covered pad is likely to give you better mounts in ultra-fast situations, but proper mounting usually allows you to use a recoil pad of rubber if you want. If your pad is sticking, varnish the sides (not the face), and it will slide along your vest or jacket better.

Gun Reliability

In every case, no matter what the use, you should buy the very best gun you can afford—always and every time. There is no piece of equipment that you can cut corners on as easily as your gun, yet it is the last one you should even consider trying to save a buck on.

Unless you have the word "sucker" painted on your forehead and spend a lot of time at gun shows, you pretty much will find that you get what you pay for when it comes to buying a shotgun, especially a double. And with the prices of auto-loaders and pumps climbing each year, a good used double often favorably competes with these repeaters.

If you find a double with nice-looking, although rolled-on, engraving for a very cheap price new, I'd suggest you beware; if a gun deal seems too good to be true, it probably is. Likewise, some of the deals on used guns are incredible. The word "Parker" on a shotgun does not justify a zillion dollars, but in some cases, that's about the going rate. Parkers were and are nice guns. I've got one and I love it. But don't spend your kid's Harvard tuition buying one.

A good double, over/under or side-by-side, is an incredibly reliable gun. I was in Mexico shooting doves once where the heat of the air and the heat from many shots fired really tested a gun. I was the only one shooting a double—the rest were repeaters—and I was the only one who didn't have anything break or jam up.

And with proper care, one will last virtually forever, regardless of who the maker is—again, provided it was a good gun to start with. One of the major problems is overlubrication. A good gun needs little in the way of oil, and nothing in the way of grease. Grease and heavy oil applications have a tendency to trap powder residue, grit, and sand or dirt. These particles have a way of working their way onto the hinge pin, against the standing breech, or some other tight spot. Then when you fire the gun, the recoil drives this foreign matter against the

critical metal parts, resulting in undue wear. Even opening and closing a gun with grit in the works wears on the parts.

Speaking of opening and closing, remember: Close a double
gently, holding the top lever to the right, then letting the lever back
until it wants to stop on its own under its own spring pressure. Slamming a gun wears it faster than anything. The gun was made for
shooting; it wasn't made for slamming shut!

A good case that will protect a gun in transit is another way to
extend a gun's life. I prefer a take-down case, even though one is a
little inconvenient if you travel from spot to spot by car during a day's
hunting. The long, sleeve-type cases protect against scratches, but I've
heard of barrels being bent if something in the trunk shifts and
pinches the gun. Even a heavy dog standing wrong on the barrels can
harm the gun.

Pumps are reliable guns, but I'm afraid I can't vouch for auto-
loaders. These guns, depending upon recoil or the gases generated by
fired shells to operate their mechanisms, have just too many parts to
go wrong for my money. Yes, autos soak up recoil, and I recommend
them for certain types of shooting, such as dove (where the action
won't be as fast as I saw it in Mexico, as noted earlier), but the simpler
actions – pumps and doubles – offer better dependability.

One thing that can affect a gun's performance over the long haul is
the choice of loads it's asked to handle, especially if the gun is used for
a variety of game and situations. In England and continental Europe,
guns are built with the shot load in mind. That is, a gun made to
handle one-and-a-quarter ounces of shot is a larger, heavier gun than
one built for one-ounce loads, even if the two guns are the same
gauge. The bigger gun will weigh more, be thicker at the grip
("hand"); the frame will have more beef and heft to it; and the felt
recoil will be reduced. Reduced also will be the chance for something
going wrong. If you consistently fired heavy shells through a light
gun, the gun would give it up, the Europeans feel, and they're right.

Yet on this side of the Atlantic, we constantly praise the light, fast
20-gauge. Try to find one that weighs less than six pounds, and then
load it up with hot, heavy loads up to and including three-inch mag-
nums, trying for 12-gauge authority with 20-gauge weight. Not only
does that usually hurt like hell if you touch it off a lot in a day, it also
isn't any good for the gun over a period of time – and not a very long
period. Frames, even of modern steel, can crack and loosen under
constant recoil from loads that are too heavy.

If you feel you need 12-gauge authority, I suggest you get a 12-
gauge. Not only will the recoil be less on your shoulder, the gun's

relative massiveness will enable it to handle the charges without undue wear or damage. And you'll like the performance of a 12-gauge load fired through a 12-gauge gun. Patterns and shot strings are much better than firing too much shot through a hole too small.

Shooting Techniques

In the uplands, as nowhere else, the shooter has the opportunity to use, variously, each of the major shooting styles. Just like a quarterback who has to know when to float a pass and when to rifle it, the accomplished shooter has to know, almost instinctively, which style to use and at what time.

The Sustained Lead

This refers to the technique that finds the gunner mounting his gun, establishing what looks like the proper amount of allowance ahead of the moving target, and then keeping that distance as he swings with the mark. After he has swung long enough so that things are going smoothly and all looks right, he triggers his shot and keeps swinging.

This style works well on targets that can be seen for some time and that are in the open—flighting doves, for example. It is a very precise form of wingshooting, but one that has little margin for error. If the gunner "rides" the bird, he may well unknowingly slow the swing so that when the shot is fired, he is behind. Also, it takes experience to recognize over a shotgun barrel the proper lead for a given mark at a given distance, moving at a given speed. Additionally, a gun with the weight more forward lends itself to this style; guns with their weight more centered or toward the rear are difficult to use this way because they are so easy to stop or slow during the important instant just before the shot is fired.

But there are times when this is the best method to use, especially, I've found, when long ranges and tight chokes are the norm, such as on doves that are skittish, or on chukars, which someone else has moved off the rimrock, diving by you at extreme—but makeable— range.

The Snap Shot

This style calls for a quick movement in which the gun is mounted, pointed, and triggered as soon as the butt touches the shoulder. In the thick brush, sometimes this is the only technique that gives us a chance. But unless the target is a dead, true, straightaway – in effect, a stationary target – we are likely to miss, because the true snap shot does not take lead or swing into account at all. Difficult to master, and needing a perfectly fitting gun, this technique is used only a very few times, because there are few true straightaways in upland gunning – most of our shots are at angles, however slight.

The Modified Snap Shot

This style calls for the speed of the true snap shot, but with some variation. That variation is the swinging of the gun along the target's line of flight in such a way that as the bird moves, the muzzles chase the bird on their way up, pass the bird as the gun is being mounted, and the shot is taken as the butt touches the shoulder. It has the speed of the snap shot, but with the swing inherent in the mounting procedure. Thus, when the shot is taken, it is taken with muzzles ahead of the bird and moving. Good brush shots have mastered this technique to the point that it is often mistaken for the true snap. This, too, is the area of shotgunning that requires an excellent gun fit, because there is little time for adjustment as there is with the sustained lead method.

The Swing Through

Sometimes called the "fast swing," this style finds the gunner mounting the gun, starting behind the bird, establishing the swing along and through the line of flight, and swinging past the bird. Then, when the muzzles have passed the mark, he fires. Usually, at the closer ranges, just passing the bird is sufficient to ensure a hit, but if the ranges are long, the gunner has to be conscious of seeing a good amount of daylight between his muzzle and the bird.

The swing through is a good technique for open-field gunning at targets – such as flushing pheasants – that appear suddenly, but that are not going to get out of range or sight easily. On some targets, such as Hungarian partridge and sharptails, this method gives some of the speed of the modified snap shot and some of the precision of the sustained lead method.

With all of these methods, the follow-through is important. In every case except the true snap shot, the barrels have to be moving in order to register a hit. One of the best places to learn these various methods and when to use them is at a sporting clays facility where the stations test not only your skill at pointing and swinging but also your skill in choosing the right style for each station [see "Clay Target Shooting Games"].

The placement of the leading, forend, hand sometimes affects the success of the shooter. The sustained lead method cries for a long hold—the leading hand well extended on the forend wood or the barrels themselves. With the methods where speed is more often needed, such as the modified snap shot, the leading hand is placed closer to the rear, providing the leverage for the quick points and swings that make this method its most effective.

The placement of this hand can also affect the way stock length feels. A stock that is a bit short, for example, can be made to feel right by taking a longer hold than normal with the leading hand, and vice versa for a stock a tad too long. Anything more drastic than "a little" should be dealt with as a stock-fitting problem.

Slumps and Misses

In any athletic activity, there are going to be slumps, sudden unexplained failures to do that which you've always done fairly well before. I've had hitting slumps when I played baseball, and I'm in the middle of a golfing slump that started twenty years ago—but I'm ready to break out of it any day now. I know it.

But the worst slump for us is the shooting slump: sudden, unaccounted-for misses on birds that we'd normally grass with little effort. Sometimes these slumps last for a whole season, sometimes for a day or part of a day. Whenever they grab you, though, you feel like that's it—you'll never hit again.

Usually a slump occurs because you are doing something slightly different. Baseball players change their batting stances without knowing it, a little each day, until they've bound themselves up and hitting drops off; basketball players forget to flex their knees on free throws and go 0-for-14 from the line. Usually the slump is mechanical in nature, but it quickly becomes mental as well, and that's the tough part to break. When we miss shots we should make, we start pressing, we tighten up, the swing slows up, and we get to miss some more.

I remember a slump I once hit while dove shooting. The birds were passing by at twenty-five to thirty-five yards, good shooting range for the improved cylinder auto-loader 20 I was shooting. They weren't flaring badly, and there was no wind. I shot, I think, four out of the first six I fired at, and then started missing—a lot.

It dawned on me that I was riding the birds, seeing them come from some distance off. I was mounting the gun prematurely and riding them instead of being aggressive with my swing. I started waiting until the birds were where I wanted them, mounted and fired quickly, and the slump ended.

Missing is part of the game, but prolonged missing is another matter—the seemingly unending string of loud noises and no feathers makes us wish we'd taken up something simple like neurosurgery-by-numbers. Usually, slumps end as mysteriously as they began, but you can shorten one by paying attention to mechanics and by concentration: not pressing and tightening up, but thoughtful consideration of the task immediately at hand.

Picking shots carefully, taking those with a high percentage of success potential, is a good way of making some shots that will get your confidence back up. You may have to pass up some of the more marginal opportunities to wait for the sure thing, but a few of these hits in a row, and you're back in there, and the slump has ended.

Some slumps that don't end can reflect another set of problems. Aging tightens joints and muscles, and a gun that once fit perfectly now does not. Usually, as we age, the perfect gun fit is one with more drop at comb and heel than we once used, as vertebrae tighten and cheeking a straight stock becomes more difficult—so we don't. Likewise, putting on or taking off weight has a drastic effect. Show me a bird shooter who has gained or lost twenty-five pounds since the previous season—or over the course of several seasons—and I'll show you a shooter whose gun doesn't fit him any longer.

An injury, obviously, hurts gun fit. Even getting some teeth yanked will create a hollow in the cheek that once was not there—the equivalent increased cast-off is now part of your gun/face relationship.

But most misses are mechanical in nature, and of these, head-lifting is the most common.

Bird flushes. Gunner mounts gun. Bird is in the open. Gunner says, "I drove all this way to shoot this bird, and I'm gonna get a good look at the whole thing." Up goes the head, the barrels rise in unison, the shot is missed. Gunner, at this point, usually curses his dog, although no one, including the dog, knows why.

Second most common—maybe tied for first—is stopping the swing. We have to follow through in any athletic activity, from hitting a baseball to throwing a bowling ball to swatting a tennis ball. The reason is, if we gear our minds to stop as soon as the act is completed, we will stop before. Golfers keep watching the tee stuck in the ground even after the club head has gone through and taken the ball away. If they didn't fix their minds to fix their eyes on the spot where the ball was, they would look up *before* the ball was struck. If you want to stop your car at the corner, when do you put on the brakes? Not *at* the corner, but *before*. Thus it is with a swinging shotgun. Unless you school yourself to continue to swing the gun through *after* the shot, you'll stop it before the proper lead has been established, or at least you'll slow it down enough to miss.

Trigger pulls can often lead to some unexplained misses, especially if the gunner either switches guns a lot, or if the pulls are too hard. A creepy, heavy trigger let-off is not very conducive to good shooting, because you are never really sure, subconsciously, when the gun is going to go off.

Trigger sears can be filed to lighten pulls, and sometimes just a good cleaning of the locks will drastically alter the weight of the pulls. I'm always a little surprised at the advice we hear about shooting triggers with such-and-such a weight. Really, the weight of the pulls should be related directly to the weight of the gun.

For example, a good rule of thumb is that the trigger, or the first trigger of a double-trigger shotgun, should let off at pressure equaling half the weight of the gun. A seven-pound 12-gauge should have its trigger set at a crisp three-and-a-half pounds. This may seem light at first, but when your shooting improves, you'll like it. A light trigger takes the "thinking" out of letting off a shot. The light pull seems to react faster, the gun seems just to shoot quicker—not dangerously so, but in the sense of its being a responsive piece. Heavy pulls, or those with a lot of trigger "play," just slow everything down.

On a double-trigger gun, especially one with a straight grip, the second trigger should let off at a weight twenty-five percent more than the first trigger. So let's say that, for the sake of the arithmetic, we are shooting a little six-pound 20 and the pulls seem heavy for such a light gun. The gun has a straight grip, meaning that the angle of the gripping hand gives more leverage on the rear trigger and you will have it set at its corresponding twenty-five percent more than the front trigger. The proper weights, then, should be: front trigger, three pounds; rear trigger, three-and-three-quarter pounds. With a straight grip, each trigger will feel the same to you because, as I said, you get a better angle on the rear trigger. If the 20-gauge has a single trigger, it should be set at three pounds.

Trigger pulls get heavier with time, and they have to be checked periodically. Trigger-pull gauges are available, but you can do the same thing if you have an accurate scale or a friendly butcher who'll let you use his.

Put snap caps in the gun, make sure it's cocked, and take a tin can and some sugar and a string. Stand the gun upright so that the butt is resting on the floor, and loop the string over the trigger, the empty can attached and hanging down a few inches but not touching the floor. Add sugar, a teaspoonful at a time, until the gun snaps. Remove the whole apparatus and weigh it—can, sugar, string, and all. Repeat a couple of times so you have an accurate figure. Then, you know if, indeed, your well-set pull is tightening up on you as time passes.

Speed

Being a fast shot seems to be important to a lot of hunters. This desire is rooted in fact: A lot of the birds we hunt, such as quail in the thick stuff, all woodcock, and all grouse, are marks that put distance between us and them in a hurry. Also, early in the hunting seasons for these birds, the cover is usually thick, so, for example, a woodcock twenty yards away might as well be in Hanoi for all the good it will do us. Last season, I was hunting grouse in the early season. I flushed thirteen birds—or had thirteen flushes, anyway—saw two birds, shot at one, and missed.

Speed also has the allure of making you talked about where the campfire burns low and shooters drag out their theories. Everyone likes to hear things like: "That Smitty is a fast hand with a gun. Bird don't hardly have a chance 't all." Makes us feel like "Bring On Wyatt Earp," right?

Speed has one additional draw, maybe the one almost nobody talks about, and that's this: Many of us—maybe even most—want to be fast in order to beat our partners to the shot, to slicker a bird right out from under his nose. Not steal his shot, mind you, but to take the bird that comes up between you and that is fair game for either shooter. There *is* something satisfying about having the bird drop at your shot a split second before your partner's pattern passes harmlessly where the bird would have been had you not been so quick, you greased-lightning little buckaroo, you.

I was shooting pheasants once with a friend of mine, Jack Morris. Now if his name is familiar, it's because he is a major league baseball pitcher. Fact is, based on overall stats like innings pitched, wins, strikeouts, and so forth, he's the best pitcher in baseball over the last ten years. Morris has superb reflexes, as you might imagine, and the highlight of my day was dropping a bird that came up fairly for both of us before he could trigger his shot. See what I mean? (Anyhow, once he caught on to the rules—that there weren't any—I didn't have a chance. But it was fun for one shot.)

Okay, so you won't give up your dream of being a quick shot, and you sure won't listen to me when I tell you that being fast should be

A couple of bird hunters admiring their guns. Left, Detroit Tiger pitching great Jack Morris; right, author's son Chris.

second to being "good," as in "hitting what you shoot at." We all know that taking a little more time adds a lot in effectiveness and you won't lose chances at birds. I can also tell you a gun with a little more weight forward will slow you down and give you a smoother swing, which helps greatly.

So, what do you have to do to be fast? Well, first, you have to be ready, and that means you have to expect a bird at any moment all day in the field. The gun has to be carried so that it can be brought into play quickly and efficiently. You have to forgo admiring the dog, looking at the autumn colors, or seeing if the honey mushrooms are out yet. You have to single-mindedly go about your business of being ready to shoot at an instant's notice, to make your move at the first sight and sound of wings.

Second, you have to use a gun that will make you quick. Weight is not *that* much of a consideration, but balance is. That means a gun with distinct muzzle-lightness, one that comes into play quickly, and one that you can snap shoot, because fast shooters are normally snap-shooters—the modified snap if they have the time, but usually just pull up and *blam*! Accuracy is way down the list of priorities.

Your reactions enter into the equation somewhere, because a slow reactor can't keep up with the guy who hit .450 on the high school baseball team three years running. You have to take what nature gave you and improve on it. Wear clothing that won't bind you or catch your gun; walk over deadfalls and depressions left foot first (if you're right-handed) so that you are always in shooting position; guard the gun barrels from branches at every turn, or else the clutching vines will slow you up.

Sounds a lot like work, doesn't it. Well, it is, and it rarely pays off, because that wild creature you are hunting has the reactions of the prey species—they have no "lag time" between stimulus and response like we do. So the truth is, if the cover is *that* thick, they haven't made the man or the gun that can beat a quail through the opening, and the human does not exist who can mount and fire when a grouse bursts out at ten feet and has only five feet to go to safety. You'll miss or, worse, cripple and not know it.

So be as fast as you have to be when the chance comes up, and don't dawdle. But don't snatch at a bird, your face off the stock and the forend hand wringing the barrels. Be smooth and efficient, and stay cool. The birds that get away because you are a little slower this way are nothing compared to those that escape because you snatch at them and throw the shot away, teeth gritted and eyes bulging.

And make an agreement with your partner that outshooting each

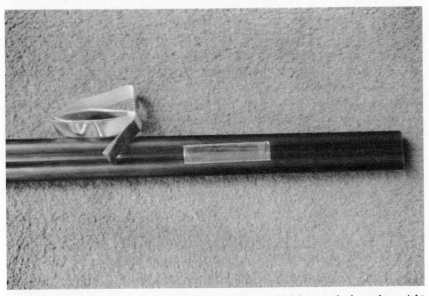

Lead tape, available at golf pro shops and used for weighting golf clubs, can also be used to weight shotgun barrels, making them temporarily heavier by a slight amount for certain uses. Often, short-barreled guns need to swing a little better in certain situations. The tape can be removed when the gun's normal balance is needed again.

other is stupid and counterproductive to a pleasant day in the field and that you are going to take it easy, not compete. You don't care what he does, but this is no contest.

Gun Configurations—by Species

I'm presenting here a series of charts that are meant to be a guide for the upland hunter when it comes time to make a choice about what gun will work the best for what species, or when he gets that acquisitive gleam in his eye for a new gun.

These charts are not meant to be etched in granite, but are guidelines; these are what are likely to work the best for the most people. For example, I recommend that the 28-gauge be used on ruffed grouse "with caution" and with due regard for range and shooting conditions. I've shot a lot of grouse with the 28—some pheasants and quail, too. But day in and day out, for most people, the 20 or 16 is going to do a better job—so will the 12, if it falls into the advised weight and shot-load parameters. Same with pheasants, to cite another example. I *know* a tightly choked 20 will kill pheasants, but the 16 does it better for most folks, and the 12 does it best, again, remembering the caution about weight and shot load.

Also, remember in making your choices that gauge, shot load, and choke are interrelated. Using pheasants as an example, we see that the 16 and 12 are recommended, the 20 with caution. So if you choose either the 20 or the 16, you should also choose the tighter chokes. If you choose the 12, capable of shooting the larger shot loads effectively, then you have some freedom to use less constrictive chokes.

Quail (Western Species)

Gun Weight: 5½ 6 6½ 7 7½
Balance: Weight forward **Weight centered** Weight rear
Gauge: 28 **20 16 12**
Barrel Length: 25 **26 28** 30
Stock: **Normal** High-shooting
Shot Size: #4 #5 **#6 #7½ #8** #9
Shot Load: ¾ oz. ⅞ oz. **1 oz. 1⅛ oz.** 1¼ oz.
*Choke(s):   Cylinder (skeet) **Improved Cylinder [Modified] Improved Modified** Full

* Any combination of choices set in bold for a double
[ ] Best all-around choke for a repeating shotgun

Quail (Bobwhites)

Gun Weight: 5½ 6 6½ 7 7½

Balance: **Weight forward**   **Weight centered**   **Weight rear****

Gauge: **+28 20 16** 12

Barrel Length: **25 26** 28 30

Stock: Normal **High-shooting**

Shot Size: #4 #5 **#6 #7½ #8** #9

Shot Load: ¾ oz.   ⅞ oz.   **1 oz. 1⅛ oz.** 1¼ oz.

*Choke(s):   **Cylinder (skeet) [Improved Cylinder Modified]** Improved Modified   Full

* Any combination of choices set in bold for a double
[ ] Best all-around chokes for a repeating shotgun
** If most shooting is in brush
+ Use with caution and regard for range

Pheasants

Gun Weight: 5½ 6 6½ **7 7½**

Balance: **Weight forward**   **Weight centered**   Weight rear

Gauge: 28 **+20 16 12**

Barrel Length: 25 **26 28** 30

Stock: Normal **High-shooting**

Shot Size: #4 **#5 #6 #7½** #8 #9

Shot Load: ¾ oz.   ⅞ oz.   **+1 oz. 1⅛ oz. 1¼ oz.**

*Choke(s):   Cylinder (skeet) **+Improved Cylinder   Modified [Improved Modified]   Full**

* Any combination of choices set in bold for a double
[ ] Best all-around choke for a repeating shotgun
+ Use with caution and regard for range

Ruffed Grouse

Gun Weight: **5½ 6 6½** 7 7½

Balance: Weight forward **Weight centered Weight rear**

Gauge: **+28 20 16 12**

Barrel Length: **25 26** 28 30

Stock: **Normal High-shooting**

Shot Size: #4 #5 **#6 #7½ #8** #9

Shot Load: ¾ oz.   + ⅞ oz.   1 oz.   1⅛ oz.   1¼ oz.

*Choke(s):   **Cylinder (skeet) [Improved Cylinder] Modified** Improved Modified   Full

* Any combination of choices set in bold for a double
[ ] Best all-around choke for a repeating shotgun
+ Use with caution and regard for range

Woodcock

Gun Weight: **5½   6   6½   7   7½**

Balance: Weight forward   Weight centered   **Weight rear**

Gauge: **28   20   16   12**

Barrel Length: **25   26**   28   30

Stock: Normal   **High-shooting**

Shot Size: #4   #5   #6   #7½   #8   #9

Shot Load: **¾ oz.   ⅞ oz.   1 oz.**   1⅛ oz.   1¼ oz.

*Choke(s):   **Cylinder (skeet) [Improved Cylinder] Modified** Improved Modified   Full

* Any combination of choices set in bold for a double
[ ] Best all-around choke for a repeating shotgun

Doves (Mourning, White Wing), in normal pass shooting situations

Gun Weight: 5½   6   6½   **7   7½**

Balance: **Weight forward**   Weight centered   Weight rear

Gauge: **+28   20   16   12**

Barrel Length: 25   26   **28   30**

Stock: **Normal**   High-shooting

Shot Size: #4   #5   #6   #7½   #8   #9

Shot Load: ¾ oz.   ⅞ oz.   **1 oz.**   1⅛ oz.   1¼ oz.

*Choke(s):   Cylinder (skeet)   **Improved Cylinder [Modified]   Improved Modified   Full**

* Any combination of choices set in bold for a double
[ ] Best all-around choke for a repeating shotgun
+ Use with caution and regard for range

Chukars

Gun Weight: 5½ 6 6½ 7 7½

Balance: Weight forward **Weight centered** Weight rear

Gauge: 28 **20 16 12**

Barrel Length: 25 **26 28** 30

Stock: **Normal** High-shooting

Shot Size: #4 #5 #6 #7½ #8 #9

Shot Load: ¾ oz. ⅞ oz. **1 oz. 1⅛ oz.** 1¼ oz.

*Choke(s):   Cylinder (skeet) **Improved Cylinder [Modified] Improved Modified Full**

* Any combination of choices set in bold for a double
[ ] Best all-around choke for a repeating shotgun

Sage Grouse

Gun Weight: 5½ 6 6½ 7 7½

Balance: **Weight forward Weight centered** Weight rear

Gauge: 28 **+20 16 12**

Barrel Length: 25 **26 28** 30

Stock: Normal **High-shooting**

Shot Size: **#4 #5 #6** #7½ #8 #9

Shot Load: ¾ oz. ⅞ oz. **+1 oz. 1⅛ oz.** 1¼ oz.

*Choke(s):   Cylinder (skeet) **+Improved Cylinder [Modified] Improved Modified Full**

* Any combination of choices set in bold for a double
[ ] Best all-around choke for a repeating shotgun
+ Use with caution and regard for range

Prairie Chickens and Sharptails

Gun Weight: 5½ 6 6½ 7 7½

Balance: Weight forward **Weight centered** Weight rear

Gauge: 28 20 **16 12**

Barrel Length: 25 26 **28** 30

Stock: Normal **High-shooting**

Shot Size: #4 **#5 #6** #7½ #8 #9

Shot Load: ¾ oz.   ⅞ oz.   1 oz.   **1⅛ oz.**   **1¼ oz.**
*Choke(s):   Cylinder (skeet)   Improved Cylinder   **Modified [Improved Modified]**   **Full**

* Any combination of choices set in bold for a double
[ ] Best all-around choke for a repeating shotgun

Hungarian Partridge

Gun Weight: 5½   6   **6½**   **7**   7½
Balance: Weight forward   **Weight centered**   Weight rear
Gauge: 28   20   **16**   **12**
Barrel Length: 25   26   **28**   30
Stock: Normal   **High-shooting**
Shot Size: #4   #5   **#6**   **#7½**   #8   #9
Shot Load: ¾ oz.   ⅞ oz.   1 oz.   **1⅛ oz.**   **1¼ oz.**
*Choke(s):   Cylinder (skeet)   Improved Cylinder   **Modified [Improved Modified]**   **Full**

* Any combination of choices set in bold for a double
[ ] Best all-around choke for a repeating shotgun

Just for the sake of fun, I tabulated all of these recommendations to see if, indeed, there *is* an all-around upland gun. I just averaged the charts and assumed that the upland shooter would, eventually, use the gun on all of the upland species I talk about. Naturally, giving equal weight value to each species of upland birds is not valid, because most of us hunt a few species of birds exclusively. Nevertheless, the results were somewhat surprising.

The best all-around gun, according to my experience and tabulations, would be:

Weight: 6½ pounds
Balance: Weight centered between the hands
Barrel Length: 26 or 28 inches
Stock: High-shooting (pattern placement about one-third pattern
      above point of aim)
Shot size: #6, #7½
Shot Load: 1⅛ ounces
Chokes: Improved Cylinder through Improved Modified (or
      screw-in chokes)
Gauge: 16

Now, there's a surprise, although to some of us, I'm sure, not a very big one: The 16-gauge, the true upland bird shooter's gun of a bygone era, is still a valid choice—maybe *the* choice as an all-around gun.

Ammunition

I would have liked to have been around during those days when a hunter sat down with his ammunition maker to discuss where he'd be hunting during the coming fall, what guns he'd be using, and what the conditions would be like in terms of distance, leaf fall, and cover.

I think that I'd have really enjoyed ordering up a batch of drop-shot 10s for close woodcock or chilled 3s for the left barrel of my tight-shooting 10 because I was a little hesitant about the ranges on my coming prairie chicken shoot out West.

In those days, ammunition was a custom-order or do-it-yourself proposition. Later, as over-the-counter shells came into vogue, there were myriad offerings by the major ammunition makers, and there were more ammunition makers. You could really pick and choose, fine-tuning your load for each species and even each barrel of a double.

But American life and business have had their way, and the loadings offered to upland shooters today are a pitiful few compared with those years. But those that are there are good indeed. Shell cases no longer swell or avoid ejection because of moisture—they're plastic—and shot collars and plastic wads have improved patterns beyond anything even our fathers could have imagined.

Shot is "chilled" by the addition of antimony, and it is possible still to fine-tune a barrel by experimenting with various loads. For example, the cheap shells intended for the upland hunter are often loaded with very soft shot, shot that deforms and thus loses its effectiveness after too many yards. This makes these shells not very useful for long-range pheasants, but in the proper shot size, they are dandy with brush birds, because these deforming shot add inches of critical pattern spread while they retain killing velocities in the very short ranges.

To show you what I mean, I'll tell you about the three woodcock I shot yesterday (honest!). All three were dead when they came down, yet none was badly shot up, even though the ranges for all three birds were under fifteen yards when I fired. Each bird had several very flat shot in them, meaning that they were taken with the edge of the pattern, an edge made wider by these deformed shot scrubbing flat against the bore and flying slightly wider than the main pattern spread of mostly round shot. Now at thirty yards, those same shot could have been cripplers or flyers, but at ten or twelve yards, they have to be considered part of the pattern. I'm going to eat the proof tonight over toast with some decent red wine.

Right now, the hardest shot made in lead is found in live-pigeon loads, usually in #7½. This stuff is expensive, but it patterns very nicely and it retains energy down range, making for good penetration and clean kills. The speed is good on these loads, and live-pigeon loads can take all but the largest of our upland birds, although in a pinch and over a good dog, I'd use them on pheasants. Hard-shot shells can be used exclusively, as the left or top barrel in a double, or as subsequent follow-up shots in a magazine gun.

Ammo companies make a lot of money on their maximum-load shells. These are fast, but they slow down fast, the laws of physics dictating that. They also contain some pretty soft shot, meaning patterns aren't what they should be in some cases. Shot collars have helped, but the best patterns come from shells with collars *and* hard shot. At extreme ranges, this is what you need.

But upland hunters don't normally test their shot-load-gun combination as much as waterfowlers do in day-to-day hunting, so most of what the companies offer is going to be good enough for us.

But it is imperative that you test your guns with the shot you'll be using to get an idea of pattern and penetration (shoot at an old phone book and count the pages the shot penetrates, then compare with a different load and a different phone book). You may find that Winchester 7½s pattern better in your barrel than do Federals, or the other way around. You may find that a good trap load of #7½ is better for you than a high-velocity #7½ because the harder shot gives you better patterns, better penetration, and it may even cost less. You may find that standard target loads of #9 skeet shells may be all you need for woodcock, and the hardness of the shot doesn't matter.

But there are some shortcomings among the ammunition we can buy, notably in the 16- and 28-gauges. These are the vagaries of volume and demand at work—not many people shoot those gauges. Still, what we have today is pretty much going to do the job if we point the gun right, and that gun is the right one for the job at hand.

8
Gear

Let's take duck hunting. The main purpose there, as far as coping with conditions, is to stay alive until it's time to go in. So that means staying warm and dry. Since movement is at a minimum most of the time, you have to dress for warmth—and then it usually isn't enough.

Upland hunters face a different set of conditions, among these the need for ventilation because we're moving almost all of the time. So upland hunters have to dress fairly light; nothing is worse than over-dressing and ending up hot and clammy. Miserable.

Another condition is the cover we plow through. Anything that can stick, scrape, and scratch you is found where upland birds of one type or another are found—we have to go in there after them, don't we? So toughness is a second requirement of our gear.

Last, we have to be able to stay mobile for the odd off-balance shot and so that we can lift our legs over the deadfalls, blowdowns, and other impedimenta the coverts provide.

I suppose this is a hell of a time to bring it up, but with all we have to go through as upland bird hunters, one of the most important pieces of gear we can have is a functional body—one that's in shape enough to take the rigors of upland hunting, especially those three- and four-day hunts out of state that we've saved for. Nothing is worse than not being able to hit the deck the next day when the birds are flying.

Now, I'm not going to lecture you about exercising—I personally try to run over runners when I'm driving down the highway (the show-offs disgust me)—but you should do something about keeping your legs in shape, or at least getting them in shape before the season. I do a lot of stream fishing in the summers, which helps, and so does walking and working my dog. I like to play golf with my two sons. I keep score and win all the time because I cheat, but the main attraction is walking eighteen holes—which is farther than the pros have to walk, because they're walking in a straight line, not back and forth like I do chasing my Dunlop.

By the end of the season, most of us are in pretty good shape, even if we hunt only one day a week—the legs are the first thing to come back into condition with a lot of use, and they're the easiest part of the body to use. But once you pass the magical age of thirty-five— and probably most of us have—then you have to give some consideration to the amount of booze, tobacco, and late nights that are part of our daily debauchery. I'd like to die in a good woodcock covert some-day—about 160 years from now—but I feel sorry for the people who'd have to lug the body out. So, I'd suggest you make sure your cardiac system is in good shape. The walk from an air-conditioned office to your air-conditioned car every day doesn't prepare you for the walk across a Texas dove field with forty pounds of gear, and it certainly doesn't get you in shape for your annual week in South Dakota chasing ringnecks.

Now, throw in on top of the exercise a dog that checks in only during months containing an "F" and guns that suddenly shoot nine feet left/right/up/down, and the frustrations of this fine autumn sport can give you a permanent vapor lock. Don't even think about trying to ship a gun by air—that'll kill you all by itself.

So watch your waistlines, guys, and try to enjoy yourselves. Above all, get some pre-season exercise so that at least you'll be alive long enough to get your money's worth out of the guns you've bought and stashed away. By the way, make sure at least *someone* knows what those guns are worth for your heirs. If you told your wife your Webley

Leather bird straps, like this one, are great for keeping birds exposed to fresh air immediately after being shot. For those who think birds taste better after being hung for a day, the strap does this as well. This strap holds a bag of Iowa pheasants; smaller versions hold smaller birds.

only cost a hundred dollars, make sure that your kid knows the real price for the estate sale.

Now, let's take a look at the actual gear. First, starting at the top, comes the hat. A hat should do some things for you besides saving the world from a view of your receding hairline. First, it should keep off the rain, and it should keep the hair out of your eyes. If the time of year is such that warmth is a problem, the hat should also hold in your body heat—most heat loss is through the head.

The hat should also not get in the way of gun mounting. The baseball-style cap often is worn in such a manner that when you cheek the gun, the bill is in the way. So, we raise our heads to get a better view, the muzzles come up, and we miss by overshooting. I wear one of these on occasion, but I prefer the regular hat with a snapped-down brim about two inches wide. The rain funnels off it, it's warm, and it stays on in cover, something grouse and woodcock hunters appreciate.

Next comes the shooting coat or vest. This piece of gear for many of us serves as a traveling suitcase in the field. In my favorite vest right now are the following: extra dog whistle, an old pipe and even older tobacco, doggie treats, Smitty treats (jelly beans), leash, shooting glasses, gloves, a little squeeze flashlight, some Band-Aids, shotgun shells, a compass (pinned on the front), an extra dog bell, and a small camera. The whole thing weighs about eleven pounds, it seems, but it carries okay.

This vest offers some warmth, but no vest is going to take the place of a good hunting coat when the wind howls at forty knots. There are, for warm-weather shooting, the vests that are really nothing more than a series of pockets suspended by, well, suspenders. The pockets usually number three, two for shells and a third in the rear for the game we optimists always expect. I've got one I use for early-season hunting that's blaze orange. I don't like it that well because the suspenders are such that they are easily pulled off my shoulders by brush. I added a leather tie to hold the suspender straps together better, but it works better as a plains vest where brush isn't as thick as it is in an eastern woodcock covert.

As far as coats go, the old canvas coat is a piece of the past, and a pretty nice piece at that. As it ages, the sun and rain bleach it until it takes on the look of experience. But, friend, it can't hold a candle to the new stuff—or maybe I should say the "new old" stuff, particularly the oiled cotton thornproof garments now being imported into this country.

In England and Scotland for a couple of hundred years, the oiled cottons have been the standby. They are light, waterproof, they breathe, and they are pretty rugged. I've got several, among them the Beaufort jacket made by Barbour of England and the Hunting Scot Hill Jacket made by Hogg's of Fife. Now when I first got these, I felt like those fellows we see in the catalogs, so I hid from people when I wore them hunting. But they are really functional. I especially like the big game pocket in the Beaufort.

These coats aren't cheap, but they'll last longer than you will, and the waterproofing is easily rejuvenated in half an hour for about five bucks, and brother are they nice. They seem to be cool when it's warm, and warm when it's cool. I even got a knee-length one for duck hunting, but I'm afraid to wear it because my duck-hunting buddies would give me a hard time.

The main problem with a gunning coat, usually, is mobility. You have to be able to swing a gun and to move your arms for balance while you're crossing a stream on a half-rotted log. Most coats won't give you this, and any coat is more binding than a vest. So most of us get a vest bigger than we need, and to stay warm, put on a sweater or something.

Really, it's best to start a little chilly. You'll warm up fast enough through exertion, and the extra weight won't be missed, foot-pounds speaking. Whether it's vest or coat, make sure the thing has a zipper that will work and buttons big enough to be handled when your fingers are numb.

Pants should also give you freedom of movement. Make mine baggy with nylon facing to turn briars. Those little chaps are nice, too, but I always feel like I'm in a rodeo when I wear them. Get lightweight pants always—add long johns if the weather warrants.

Boots—if Gettysburg was fought over shoes, things haven't gotten much better. I love those Bean-type boots with the leather uppers and rubber bottoms, but I can't wear them because they have very little ankle support, and I've got bad ankles—like bone-surgery-three-times bad. So I wear leather boots, lace them up tight, and take in water like the *Andrea Doria*. I have those greased up and ready each season, and the grease lasts twelve seconds.

I won't bore you about socks and things like that, but I will mention some other gear that really makes things easier. First, you should get a gear bag—preferably with a shoulder strap—to hold your extras, like a lunch, shells, thermos, and so forth. Mine has that stuff, plus a dog first-aid kit with medications, tape, hemostats, and a good first-aid guide for emergency field treatments. You can buy these commercially, or you can have your vet make one up for you. If I'm going to be away from the car any distance at all, I stick this kit into my game bag and take it with me.

Shooting glasses are tough if you don't wear glasses normally. I don't, and they bother me, but not as much as a scratched cornea would, so I wear them. Two friends of mine have lost entire shooting seasons due to getting twigged, which is almost as bad as losing the eye, but not quite. Yellow or vermilion lenses heighten contrast and brighten things up so that you can pick up a bird against a brown background faster. By the way, the yellow glasses are great for night driving, too.

If you are fortunate enough to have the wherewithal to get one, a "shooting car" is a great addition because it's so practical. You can keep in it your dog crates—travel cages, that is—extra gear, a change of clothes in case you float your hat in a stream in woodcock cover, and maybe a portable grill for a *real* midday lunch.

The four-wheel drive vehicle has long since reached the state of civilization that allows it to see duty this way for a couple of months of the year yet not get you drummed out of the neighborhood association for driving it the remaining ten. Likewise, bigger carry-all units like a Chevrolet Suburban are nice-looking, although a little heavy on gas.

The shooting car can also be your little haven. If it smells like wet dogs and tobacco smoke and maybe a touch of grog now and then from when you had to sleep in it because you got lost, then your teenage kid isn't likely to borrow it for a date. Additionally, you can put stuff in there and it'll stay there because nobody's going to mess with it. A station wagon makes a pretty good hunting vehicle because it holds a lot, but it leaves something to be desired as far as traction goes, although if you can't get in and out in a wagon, maybe you ought not to be there in the first place.

I've got a wagon, and I have a wooden box in it—got it from an outdoor equipment cataloguer—with a top shelf and a spacious undersection that holds all the stuff I figure I'll need, including dry boots and socks. You can just toss stuff in it, then put it into the car and forget about it until you need it.

There are any number of public areas across this country where a bird hunter can drive in, camp for a few days, and enjoy hunting the surrounding areas—even if you pay a farmer a few bucks to let you use the back eighty. It's fun in the early fall, not so fun as winter approaches. But car camping has the advantage of being cheaper and less bothersome than full-blown tent camping.

If you travel a lot for your hunting and have spent a fortune on motels, the best solution is probably a travel trailer, camper, or some other type of conveyance—maybe even a motor home. These can be totally devoted to shooting, and your motel is right there. The only problem is, in the case of the motor home and the camper, they just don't take forest roads too well. The travel trailer, on the other hand, can be unhooked and left at your chosen spot while you use the towing vehicle as transportation.

Years ago, my father and I used to travel every year to Nebraska to hunt pheasants and quail, and we always pulled his small house trailer. We could cook, sleep, watch TV, and stay warm inexpensively. We'd park the unit at a public park and use the car to get about. After summer is over, most state parks and other recreational areas that cater to campers are deserted, so the bird hunter—unless he has to compete with deer hunters where the seasons overlap—has his choice of spots.

Accoutrements for the Gun

Your upland bird guns perform their best, and you feel your best about them, when they are accompanied by some little niceties made to, well, make them perform better.

One of these little gadgets is a leather handguard for a double with a splinter forend. Made of spring steel covered with high-grade leather, the handguard has been used for years in England to protect the shooter's hand from the heat of barrels that have grown hot from much shooting during a driven-bird hunt. These handguards perform the same function here, although only dove hunting is likely to heat up your barrels. However, since the proper place to grip the swinging end of a double is on the barrels, handguards make a nice, firm platform for holding on.

Snap caps are dummy cartridges made from brass, or even plastic, with reinforced spring-supported primers. These primers cushion the firing pins of a shotgun so that hammers can be safely snapped for dry firing or for testing trigger pulls.

Brass oil bottles are nice touches, too, although perhaps a bit impractical these days unless you carry your gun in an oak-and-leather case. Like rosewood striker (firing pin) boxes, these are more of an affectation—but a nice one—than a functional piece of equipment.

A cartridge bag, however, is a good idea. Carried on a strap around the shoulder, it can be toted to and from the field or to and from the car. It carries your shells, both the live and spent rounds, in relative cleanliness.

A sight on a shotgun is supposed to be superfluous. Well, I like a nice big white one that I can see when I'm shooting. I know all about focusing on the bird out there and not on the end of the barrels, but I still see the sight when I'm shooting, and a white one is a good reference point. If a gun is shooting a little high for you, sometimes just adding a large sight lowers impact, because we have a tendency to shoot lower to compensate for the larger reference point—the bead.

Gun cases come in a variety of styles. The easiest and cheapest are the full-length sleeve cases. They protect a gun from scratches, but there's nothing structural to stop a heavy weight from bending your barrels. They are great, though, for sliding the gun into as you make short automobile trips from cover to cover.

The leg-o-mutton case allows you to take the gun apart and carry it in safety. These cases are expensive, and most of them are in rough shape from years of use, new ones being custom jobs.

The oak-and-leather case is a fine way to keep, protect, and display a fine firearm, but it too is expensive. Some guns, like the Parker Reproduction, come so encased when you buy them; others have the cases made for them by the manufacturer and are available at extra

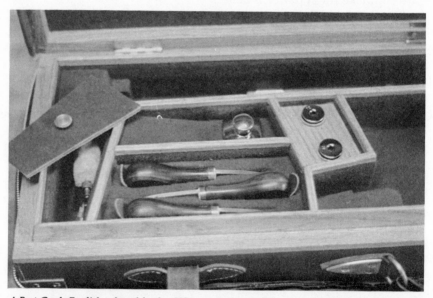

A Best Grade English oak-and-leather VC case. Such cases have long been part of the mystique of a Best Grade English gun. This one, with its snap caps, oil bottle, and turnscrews, also holds cleaning fobs and a rosewood rod. Nick Makinson of Komaka, Ontario, a transplanted English gunmaker, built this model. In some instances, a fine case such as this is priced higher than what Americans are used to paying for a gun.

For the double user, a couple of little-used but convenient accessories: snap caps and a handguard. The snap caps are used to cushion firing pins during dry-firing or for testing trigger pulls. The snap caps are also used when the hammers are "dropped" before long periods of storage, preventing hammer spring weakness. The handguard is a movable piece of spring steel covered with fine leather, and is useful when a double has a splinter forend and the shooter's hand extends at least partially past the wood—as it should. Barrels have a tendency to heat up quickly, and gadgets such as this serve a practical purpose, especially when shooting is fast, as on flighting doves or at sporting clays.

cost. The nice British models feature the gun company's emblem on the inside of the lid, and they carry enough cleaning equipment that they become a traveling cleaning station while you're in the field. There are a number of companies that make these on a custom basis, with the cost running several hundred dollars.

Since we all know that a bird hunter headed for another state with his shotgun is a threat to national security and is probably plotting the overthrow of the Republic, traveling by air with a firearm is tricky, but it can be done.

First, the gun must be encased in a sturdy carrier. I have a steel case that holds two guns that are disassembled. This case is lined with foam and felt and holds the guns snugly so that even the most determined baggage masher has a tough time making things inside rattle together.

Next, this case must be checked through as baggage, and a special red tag is placed on it, a tag that you sign attesting to the fact that the gun is unloaded and no ammunition accompanies the gun—the air-lines don't want the gun and ammunition together where some nutso can grab them and make naughty on the innocent. Shells can be carried in other baggage, but it's complicated—besides, they're heavy to lug around. I suggest buying your shells at the end of the line rather than taking them with you.

If you want to travel with guns by air and you don't have a case yet, consider getting the kind that carries your guns disassembled. Last year Tom Huggler and I were headed for Georgia to hunt quail, and I had two guns in my double, take-apart case, while Tom carried two in a double, full-length case. Tom got checked at both airports; that is, he had to open the case for inspection. I told the agent that mine were disassembled, and I had no problem. In fact, there weren't even any raised eyebrows. By the way, the Atlanta airport seems to be filled with bird hunters who serve you with a smile. Likewise the Denver airport (Stapleton). The rest look at you like you're a regional vice president of the PLO when you show up with a gun case.

For your firearms, I strongly suggest a good insurance policy that will replace the guns if they're lost, stolen, or destroyed. My pal Jim Geary, an insurance agent, tells me that scheduling these as personal property on an inland marine insurance policy is the way to go. I trust him and just pay up, but these policies are great, cheap protection for your fine guns (and cameras, your wife's jewelry, and other stuff that thieves grab first).

Some homeowner's policies protect your possessions by offering replacement if something happens—nothing prorated. In any event, you should have a separate listing of your guns with their serial numbers recorded and photographs of each. You may even want to have appraisal slips from a gunsmith or dealer. That way, when the time comes for the insurers to write you a check, there's no question on what they put right after "Pay to the Order of You."

Stashing guns in the house is tricky. Wives and burglars know where to look. The best, albeit expensive, solution is a gun safe. These safes are built like Fort Knox, and they keep thieves away. I hate going away thinking someone may clean me out, and a safe at least gives me some peace of mind.

The usual B & E man wants to get into your house, grab your stuff, and be out in under five minutes. He breaks a window, gets in, takes the obvious valuable stuff he can fence, and lights out. This crash-and-dash specialist is discouraged if he can't find your guns readily, or if your valuables are locked up tight in something that will take him an hour to scalp. Make it tough on him.

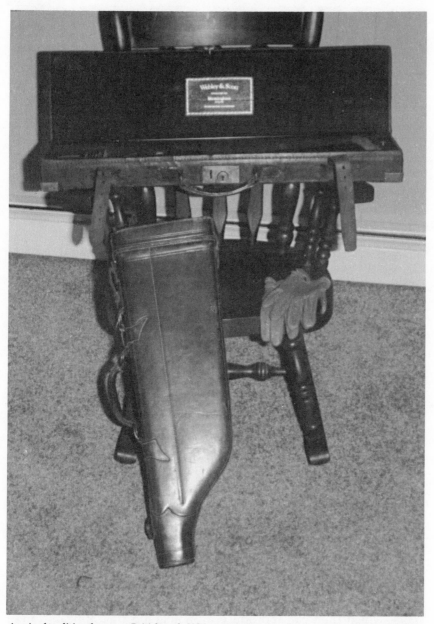

A pair of traditional cases: a British-style VC case and a leg-o-mutton case. The VC case is leather with brass corners, all over oak, and has compartments to make it a mobile cleaning station, while the leg-o-mutton case, also leather, holds the gun with little room for any cleaning accouterments. Both cases carry the guns disassembled, the safest way.

A steel-sided airplane case with tags still intact. Contrary to popular opinion, it isn't too hard to travel by air with firearms, so long as you check them through first with your other baggage. This case is padded with foam and carries a pair of doubles—the barrel and forend assemblies are stored in a lower compartment of the case. The tags are, left to right, owner identification, airline destination tag, and federal firearm tag, which the owner signs attesting to the fact that the firearms are unloaded and no ammunition is in the case. Some ticket agents ask to inspect the guns, others don't. If you travel by air, resist the urge to take your gun in a long case fully assembled—the chance of damage is greater, and you'll probably have to open the case for inspection more often.

Another good burglar stopper is a nice big bird dog with some moxie. My female, Jess, puts up a real fuss when someone comes to the door, but she's a mushbucket. Her nephew, Parker, however, weighs seventy pounds, is all muscle, and he'll bite you—lots of times and hard. He doesn't say anything at all to a stranger while Jess is yowling. He just stands there with his Clint Eastwood face on and waits. My UPS guy throws stuff at the porch from the street.

For the upland hunter, collecting maps of places he goes and areas he hunts helps a lot—sometimes we just can't find that covert again. Toward that end, topographical maps are the greatest aid of all. These are maps made up from aerial photos. The cameras used take several shots, which then can reproduce a photograph that appears three-dimensional. From these photos, the maps are drawn—not three-dimensional, but with lines that tell the elevation of an area. They are incredibly simple to read, and tell, besides elevation, the location of waterways, marshy areas, lakes and ponds, and any buildings that were in place when the aerial survey was conducted.

All roads are shown and named as well, making these dandy for when you get lost—and you will. The maps come in a size large enough so that you can see detail (the size most useable is known as the "7½-minute quadrangle"), and they are available for most of the United States for a nominal charge.

If you want maps for areas east of the Mississippi, write Eastern Distribution Branch, U.S. Geological Survey, 1200 S. Eads St., Arlington, VA 22202; for places west of the Big Muddy, write Western Distribution Branch, U.S. Geological Survey, Building 41, Federal Center, P.O. Box 25286, Denver, CO 80225.

These maps come in handy, I've found, for locating hunting spots. For example, the maps show the existence of what are called "intermittent streams," streams that are present during wet times of the year. I've found good woodcock coverts by checking out intermittent streams that pass through gaps in hilly terrain, the reasoning being that the birds while migrating are going to follow the low areas where

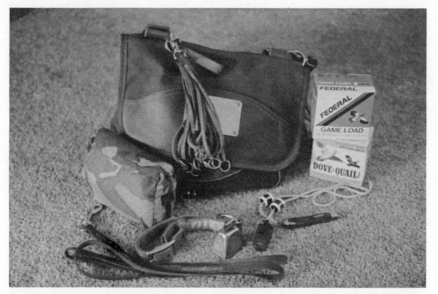

A day bag for upland hunting. The canvas-and-leather case holds, clockwise: shells, dog whistle with flush counters, pocket knife, bell and collar, lead, and dog first-aid kit. Bird loops for smaller birds are attached to the bag. The whole thing is slung over the shoulder and carried to the car with ease.

Don Chilcote, regional representative with the Ruffed Grouse Society, checks over maps of coverts he's marked. Maps can be laminated and grease pencils used to indicate things you want to remember—like, "Bull in this pasture still living!"

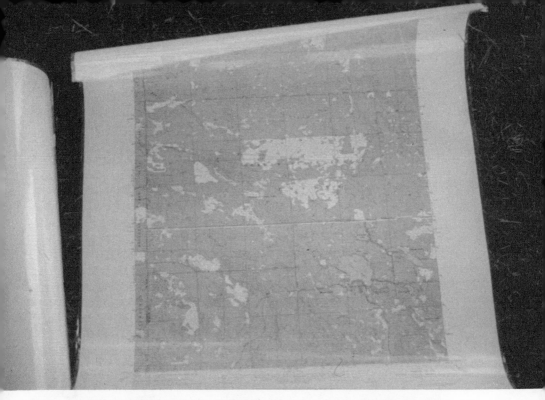

Topographic maps, available from the U. S. Geological Survey and some state agencies, show land formations and natural features as well as some roads and buildings—great for locating coverts in unfamiliar territory.

food is present. And if the fall has been dry, so much the better, because these areas are the most likely to hold food for the birds.

Likewise, topo maps can help locate potential dove-hunting areas by showing spots that may be farm fields or weed fields not visible from the road. If you are seeing doves trading back and forth, the topo maps can help you figure out where they're going to or coming from, and you can plan your place of interception better.

I like to get my topo maps laminated at an office supply store—costs two bits—and then make notations on them with a grease pencil, which can be wiped off easily if I'm wrong or want to change the notes.

These maps can be rolled up and stored in some kind of tube and carried in your car. You can never tell when they might come in really handy.

9

Clay Target Shooting Games

In this country right now, if you want to be a crack shot on clay targets, you don't have to look too far to find a facility that will take you in. If you want to be a crack *field* shot, clay targets are about the only way to learn, but the ways that clays are shot now—for the most part—only teach you the basics of becoming a good clay-target shooter.

Don't get me wrong, the shooting of clay targets is a fine way to get to know the handling characteristics of your guns, the elements of swing, lead, the follow-through, and it provides a measurable score that will show if you're improving and by how much.

But the American games of skeet and trap, as they are most commonly practiced in this country, are games that have become an end in themselves.

Originally developed to provide shooting for the landed gentry of England during the off season, or when game was scarce, trap started off as pigeon shooting in which pigeons—live ones—were released from under top hats by someone pulling an attached string. The bird then, hopefully, took off, and the shooter took a pop or two at the departing target. Later, although some live-pigeon shooting continued and continues today, the game replaced the pigeons with glass balls (filled with feathers—for the satisfaction factor, I guess), which were launched like stones from a catapult. Then, the invention of the first clay disk helped shortly to make this game what it is today. The target takes off quickly and, for the most part, doesn't slow down until it's already out of range. It has to be led, and it has to be shot swiftly. The oscillating trap helped to take the predictability out of the shooting, so the trap shooter has to be prepared for anything.

But the guns and the methods bear as much resemblance to everyday field shooting as I do to common decency—about the same as Richard Petty's race car compares to a showroom model of the same name. Trap today is shot with the gun in the fully mounted position. The target is called for and the "bird," as it's called, emerges instantly (if it doesn't, the trap boy has some explaining to do), and the shooter quickly fires his one shell from his, probably, full-choked trap gun. He stands sixteen yards away from the traphouse. If he's good, he must move back various distances and shoot with others of his ilk—the "handicap."

The angles of the birds as they leave the traphouse, however, are very interesting indeed for the upland hunter, especially the man who hunts behind a dog. The targets leave the house at angles that approximate those departing birds would take, and therein lies some of the lure of this sport for the upland hunter.

The game is funny; you shoot at targets resembling, in their flights, departing upland birds, but you use a gun that, if it has a close relative, would be like a gun used in long-range pass shooting at geese.

Trapshooting becomes a viable form of upland hunting practice when you combine the elements of upland shooting with the existing traps and facilities. For example, let's say that you are getting ready for the upcoming quail season. You want to get out your favorite 20 and get in some preseason shooting to forestall the crazies and to sharpen your eye. Well, head for the trap range when things are slow and ask if you can have some indulgence for half an hour or so. Then get yourself someone to pull the birds ("pull," by the way, is a vestige from the days when the string was pulled, the hat tipped over, and the pigeon flapped away), and stand up behind the trap house about fifteen feet from the mouth of it, hold your gun low, and start calling for the birds.

The oscillating trap takes away the advantage of knowing where the birds are coming from, and holding the gun at the ready position as you would when approaching a dog on point means you have to perform the entire wingshooting drill of mount, overtake, fire, and follow-through. Also, being closer to the house, you have more gentle angles on the right- and left-hand birds, ones that from sixteen yards appear almost as crossers. These angles are more like those bird hunters encounter in normal shooting.

And, being up close, the targets rise at angles that are more like those birds take when they spring from the ground. There is not the optical illusion of the "elevator" bird that you would encounter, again, if you were shooting from sixteen yards.

Now, at this point you can have some fun with the trap kid. Tell him to pull the birds when you've loaded your gun, but not to tell you when—the unexpected release of the bird is much more natural, and the *clunk* of the trap takes the place of the whirring of wings you hear before you see the bird.

Skeet shooting in America is even more of a groove game than trap. The shooter knows when and from where the bird will emerge, how far he has to lead it to break it, and what score he has to shoot to be in the money—or await a shootoff. Skeet was first designed by William Harnden Foster, a grouse hunter, magazine editor, artist, and author of the classic work on ruffed grouse, *New England Grouse Shooting*. Originally, the game was shot with one trap throwing the target from ground level up, as today's skeet low house does. The shooters traveled in a circle from station to station around the trap. This gave them chances at all angles from incomers to outgoers, and Foster named it "shooting around the clock."

But a neighbor—a farmer, I think—complained that Foster and his cronies were sprinkling either himself or his livestock—I forget which—with bird shot, so there ended up being one direction that they couldn't shoot. So to give the angles that were opposite the only safe ones they could shoot, they installed a second trap at the other end of the field, and the modern configuration was born.

Foster's magazine held a contest to name the new game, and "skeet" won, a word that means "to shoot" in a Scandinavian language. Thus was born the sport.

But Bill Foster would spin in his grave if he saw how his game has changed. Initially, the bird was released for a shooter who waited with the gun down. Today, the gun can be mounted as the shooter waits, and I've seen some shooters go through some mighty strange physical shenanigans getting ready. Allowing the gun to be mounted as in trap took away the necessity for a light, well-balanced piece, and now most skeet guns are too heavy for use afield, many of the stocks are too long, and the shooter would have a hard time with flushing quail or woodcock with them. It's sort of sad that the guns skeet champs use would have no chance in the grouse coverts, remembering that skeet was invented to help grouse hunters.

In the early days, when you still had to mount the gun, swing, and break the target, some of the best American gunmakers put out special skeet models. Parker, L. C. Smith, Winchester with its Model 21—all of these made skeet models, many of them, such as the Parker, sporting straight grips. Once mounting the gun was removed from the rules, the guns changed.

I don't know too much that can be done to change skeet back to what it once was, and I'm sure that those who bend the most primers at this sport every year could hardly care less what I think anyway, so it's a moot point. But if you want to sharpen up for bird hunting at a traditional American skeet field, I suggest you shoot according to the International Skeet Shooting rules—gun down and delayed birds. In international skeet, there is a built-in timer that delays the release of the bird for up to three seconds from the time you call for it, and nobody knows when or how long the delay will be. The puller can do the same thing for you if you want. Remember, the thing you want to do is be more or less surprised when a bird emerges: Practice the full drill of mount, swing, overtake, and follow-through, and get familiar with your gun again—or maybe learn how a new one handles.

For the bird hunters in America, there is a new game, one I predict is going to become the standard in this country as it already is in Britain and in places on the Continent: sporting clays. This game is one that closely resembles the situations and conditions in which upland hunters and waterfowlers operate.

There are, right now, precious few sporting clays operations or facilities in this country, but that will change. Already some big money is looking at the widespread introduction of this game into the metro centers of the United States, and one such facility is operating in Houston, Texas. The United States Sporting Clays Association (USSCA) has held its first meetings, and this embryonic organization will grow very quickly.

The attraction to sporting clays is that it so closely parallels the shooting opportunities the average hunter is familiar with. The shooting grounds themselves are set in woods (or some other cover) that closely approximate "wild" conditions. There are a number of stations, each of which presents targets—usually international-style hard targets that can withstand the force necessary to propel them at great speed—from a variety of angles that make the shooter feel he is right in the field, shooting at live birds.

For example, let's take a look at a sporting clays set-up. One station might be a "flushing pheasant" chance, in which a simple straightaway target is presented, similar in its flight path to a low-house target in skeet. By shooting at the target from a variety of angles—perhaps expending ten or twelve shells in the process—the shooter gets a thorough workout on this target. Lastly, a pair of doubles is thrown, the shooter loading and shooting two shells at these.

Another station may be the "wood duck honey hole," in which clays, thrown from an unseen trap, drop down through the treetops and have to be taken before they "land" only yards in front of the shooter. Another station is the "driven pheasant" station, in which the target comes out of an oscillating trap and zooms overhead at various angles—it looks like an aspirin twenty-five yards up.

The "driven grouse" station resembles the chances you'd get while standing behind a stone butt or blind in Scotland shooting at

Gene Hill tries for a double on "driven grouse," one of the stations at a sporting clays facility near Houston, Texas. The stones in front of Hill approximate the stone butts that are traditional in Scottish shoots. The targets emerge quickly and, because of the use of an oscillating trap, at angles unknown beforehand. In the background of this photo is visible the "pit blind" used to simulate overhead, incoming waterfowl.

Author (right) asks Bob Brister (left) and Gene Hill (center) where the shot went from the shell he just fired, because there obviously was none in it! Brister starts to talk about lead and smooth swing. Hill, who knows the author better, saves his breath.

red grouse as they wing over, only these are from an oscillating trap. The same trap, with the shooter in a pit blind dug into the ground, becomes a goose shoot at passing waterfowl.

The possibilities are endless, and there's no "grooving in." (At one shoot I was in, a certain station proved too easy the first day, so those running the shoot just changed that station the next day.) And, the gun must be held below the level of the elbow, there are delays, and some stations even require you to be able to load your gun fast—shoot at two targets, four seconds to reload, and two more are released. The organizers of the shoot I mentioned above even cooked up a "covey rise" trap that threw four clays; choose two to break.

When I've shot sporting clays, and my experience is limited, I've noticed that those who have done a lot of target shooting in traditional American trap and skeet did not fare as well as those who have hunted a wide variety of gamebirds. Bob Brister, the famous gun writer, and I talked about this in Houston, and we're both convinced that sporting clays is the wave of the future in this country for target shooting. The best part is, the set-ups allow you to work on the shots that are giving you problems. Unlike trap and skeet, the folks in-

The "pheasant tower" at a sporting clays facility, used to simulate driven pheasants or high, overhead doves. The same trap is used with the shooters rotating around it to give a greater variety of angles.

volved with sporting clays are less likely to insist on quiet. Fact is, there is usually some teasing going on that could get you a faceful of knuckles at the Grand American.

One of the delightful things about sporting clays is the lack of perfection—nobody's going to get them all. If the event looks like a marathon, the organizers are likely to change things around on your second turn. For example, I shot in the U.S. championships one year, and the winning score was 88 out of 100. I didn't win, place, or show, by the way. But I was there.

At a sporting clays shoot, the choice of gauge or gun action is entirely up to you. I saw more London Best guns at Houston than I have ever seen in use in one place in my life. I asked some of the shooters about that, and most remarked that they used these guns here, rather than in the field, because it was a good chance and place to get some mileage out of them without all the potential problems of carrying their fine guns into the field. The winner of the event, by the way, used an auto-loader, and I remember that third place went to a taped-at-the-grip Model 12 Winchester pump. With gauge open, and with prizes and money on the line, I saw nothing but 12-gauges—I

Gene Hill showing proper form on a rising, right-to-left target. Sporting clays scores are nowhere near those of regulation trap and skeet, which require perfection. Scores of 85 X 100 will win a big shoot, and the man with the bird-hunting experience has the upper hand.

168 *Hunting Upland Gamebirds*

wonder if there's a message there.

One item that has gained in popularity among those who shoot sporting clays is the screw-in choke concept. In England, where sporting clays really got started, and where it is the number one shooting sport in terms of participants and shells expended, screw-in choked double guns are about the only thing you'll see.

The reason, of course, is that the shots presented by each station can vary widely in range. On some shots, the bird must be broken quickly and at short range—as little as ten or fifteen yards; other chances call for long shots—long when you consider the size clay disks present at twenty-five yards; they look like BBs. And sometimes stations present straightaway targets that only show the edge-on profile of a target, so even though the range may be short, a dense pattern is needed to ensure a break.

The rules as they are being set up by the USSCA call for the participants to change chokes if they wish, but not after anyone on

A shooter in the "ready" position calls for his target—but he probably won't get it right away. The puller (left) has a delay built into the release switch that can trigger the trap immediately or with up to a three-second delay. The gun must be held so that the butt is visible below the elbow. This shooter's mount has already started. Doubles, many of them side-by-sides, are common at sporting clays shoots, whether in a tournament or just tuning up for the season to come. This is the most popular of all shooting games in England and could become the same here.

their squad has been called to shoot. So, the chokes must be changed in transit to the next station. As the game gathers popularity, I would expect that rule to change because of the confusion it causes. Once it becomes as widespread as I expect it to be, there will be more and more shooters using the special sporting clays guns that are marketed presently in continental Europe and England. Advertising in one English magazine touts the virtues of a special over/under, made especially for sporting clays, using screw-in chokes—it's a Winchester.

Those devoted to sporting clays are normally folks who take care with gun fit. Unlike the games where guns are pre-mounted, sporting clays place emphasis on mounting. If the gun does not fit you, you are at a disadvantage; there's no mashing down of the cheek, deep breathing, snuggling up to the stock (sounds a little perverted, really), and then calling for the bird. This is mount-and-fire shooting, and the man with a gun that fits and some bird-hunting experience behind him is the man who will do well.

At one championship, I saw live-pigeon shooters, international skeet and trap shooters, American-style skeet and trap competitors, and bird hunters who had probably shot at a dozen clays in their whole lives. The bird hunters held their own and did well. Of these groups, the American-style skeet and trap men seemed to be at the biggest disadvantage, with the live-pigeon shooters, on the whole, a bit ahead of the game—but not a whole lot.

10

The Future

The future of upland hunting in the United States is tied to a few things, the first of which is the birds themselves. The habitat that is eaten up each year is considerable, but there are bright spots, such as the potential Farm Bill acreage that is being taken out of production yearly, which could mean long-term betterment of habitat.

The future also depends upon the next generation of hunters, our sons. These youngsters are required, in most states, to take hunter safety courses before the first licenses are granted to them. These courses are great, because they teach safety and such things as the rudiments of game management. There is also considerable emphasis on ethics and the hunter's role in society and how the public views that role. Let's hope that these new hunters do a better job of portraying us than some of the hunters from past generations, so that hunting remains viable and that the anti-hunters—now in a holding pattern and no longer on the offensive—won't again have reason to point the bloody finger at us.

To carry this on a bit, many of you will say that a hunter's best partner is his dog; I prefer the partner whom you would probably consider a close second—a kid.

Most of us learned to hunt from a father, uncle, older brother, or a very generous "elderly" friend. A few of us took it up late in life. And not all of us were lucky enough to get the best instruction about the ways of birds and dogs and shotguns. And those lessons were usually learned the hard way—by learning from our mistakes.

So, like any training manual, I'd like to tell you, as a father and ex-teacher, the methods I used to take a boy—my son Chris—from pup to broke partner. He's not finished yet, because he needs more experience, but then how many of us are?

Developing the Interest

Sadly, a lot of people tell me they can't understand a youngster's lack of enthusiasm for hunting, given their own. Upon questioning, they usually reveal that the child was introduced to the outdoors at a fairly late age, say twelve or thirteen. By that time, puberty may have begun, and the boy is more interested in girls and school functions or football, an autumn sport that takes time from hunting.

I started taking Chris on short hunts when he was six. True, he was sometimes a nuisance because I had to watch out for him; I made sure the branches didn't snap back in his face and so on. At first I only took him along, then later with a close hunting partner and his son, a boy Chris's age. Together we tried to make sure the boys had pleasant days afield. At the first sign of weariness, we wrapped it up for the day. Nothing takes the edge off sharpening interest like wearing the kid to a nubbin. Many a man does this to get his son ready for the "stout life" or something equally Neanderthal. Hunting is recreation and should be treated as such.

I allowed Chris to participate in all aspects of the hunt. Introducing a child to death after he's watched Disney for most of his life is a little dicey. I suggest you quickly dispatch cripples to curb squeamishness. An imperative at all times is to call attention to television fallacies such as bears being big guys in fuzzy coats.

Have the child watch as you clean your birds after the hunt. Be ready for some youthful grimacing, but have the child help get the bird ready for the table and enjoy a meal. This helps show that the bird you shot is not much different from the chicken Mom buys. When I taught school, I was always flabbergasted by the number of kids who never stopped to think that hamburger comes from a cow that someone, somewhere, had to kill. Amazing.

Introduction to Shooting

As the youngster grows, make sure that all the lessons of gun safety are not only taught, but practiced. Having Chris help me clean my gun after a hunt made him familiar with it. So when the time came to start shooting, he knew which end to point.

I started off small: a .22 rifle at the range and tin cans filled with water. When struck, these targets sail into the air in a satisfying manner. And there is, of course, no recoil. Chris regularly accompanied me to the skeet range, and this bit of rifle shooting made him itch for more.

His eagerness was satisfied by shooting at his first moving targets. I used toy balloons, inflated and knotted, blowing across the surface of a woodland pond. The gun was that now-familiar .22 loaded with birdshot. This miniature shotshell holds enough #12 shot to do the job on a hapless balloon and splash the water with authority, still sans recoil—and the danger of ricochet. But what about the challenge? Hitting balloons scooting across a pond on a puff of wind isn't as easy as it sounds. You should try it.

From this practice, repeated often, Chris learned to swing and lead, and throw a pattern with fine shot. He made the transition from rifle aimer to swinger and pointer very nicely.

When the time came for a shotgun of his own, I bought Chris a 20-gauge youth model single barrel made by Winchester, the Model 37A. (He was eight years old, admittedly young; your child may be ready sooner or later than that.) This gun is heavy enough to soak up recoil, has a pad on the butt of the stock, and all dimensions are youth-sized so it's easy to handle. Also, it had a tight modified choke, meaning he had time to get on and still have the bird in range.

His first shots were again at those balloons using powder-puff #9 skeet loads. The recoil didn't bother Chris at all. He sort of liked that satisfying jab in the shoulder.

The next summer, at age nine, we started his shooting training in earnest at the skeet range. I took him to the club and we set up at station 7, shooting the low house. This is a going-away target with no swing or lead involved. He shot about ten times, powdering the last three clays, and that was it for the day. The next trip, we shot a box of shells at the same target; the next time, we shot a few low houses and the remainder of a box at the high house (incoming) target. This shot necessitates some lead, swing, and follow-through, actions we talked about at length—in "grown-up talk"—at home in my den.

Because of fear of recoil, most people start their youngsters off with a .410, which I think is a mistake. This gun is for the real expert and has no application in the uplands for a child. Better to start with a heavy 20-gauge and let the kid hit something. If he's hitting, he doesn't feel recoil—you don't, do you?

Also, a hard-to-define variable enters in here—a kid's coordination. My son is a good shortstop, averages ten points a game on the junior high basketball squad as a guard, and on a dead run can catch a football as hard as I can throw it. He's a natural athlete. If that sounds like bragging on my kid, it's not; I'm just saying that he was easy to teach. Plus, if there's a way to shoot wrong, I've done it in the twenty-five years I've been chasing birds. Thus, I was able to discuss with him knowledgeably such things as lead, the necessity of keeping the gun moving, gun fit, and sight picture. Maybe you'll have to back up a bit if you're one of those who just points and shoots and things drop from the sky.

Up to then all of Chris's shooting had been with the gun up and in position. The next phase was at the old station 7 with the gun down. Chris saw right away that the mounting of the gun threw him off, and he missed regularly. Dry mounting at home with his gun (as I watched) made him more familiar with the wingshooter's drill of mount, swing, lead, fire. We returned to the range, and soon he was again popping birds with the same regularity.

Time to move on to the trap range. I arranged for Chris and me to visit up behind the trap house with the boy who would pull for us. The oscillating trap throws its target in a direction unknown beforehand, so Chris couldn't lock in as he was doing at the skeet range. It was now necessary for him to see the target well as he mounted, and most shots required small amounts of lead. I explained that this is about how a bird comes out from under a dog's point, which got him excited. By the time he was powdering these targets well, it was late winter and Chris was ten.

Game Shooting

At that time we were living in Iowa, where no age restrictions on hunting were as yet in effect. Dave Meisner and I took Chris to a shooting preserve for his first bird shooting on pheasants and quail. Dave was dog handling; I was boy handling. The first bird Chris shot at was a miss, from shooting too quickly. It did him a lot of good to stand there with an empty gun while I said, "Son, you shot too soon," and then shot the bird myself. One huge fault we all have is firing too quickly. I was teaching him early to conserve effort—that he had more time than he thought.

His first bird was a high, crossing rooster pheasant, thirty-five yards out and with the wind. Chris pulled up, and I was watching over his shoulder, exhorting him to lead more. At his shot, the bird flinched, flew another twenty yards, then collapsed. Meisner took a photo of us walking back with that bird, one of my most cherished possessions.

That day Chris shot another pheasant, and when a surprise covey of quail jumped, Chris and I puffed two birds side by side going away at the same time. What a day!

Time passed. Chris was then twelve and we were living in Michigan. His first season was upon us. He graduated to a 20-gauge double, about seven pounds to soak up recoil, and we broke clays all summer. We scouted our coverts for grouse and woodcock, worked the dogs to a frothing frenzy of excitement, and with the September opener upon us, Chris couldn't sleep. He was up at 4:30 in the morning looking for me. I was drinking coffee, as pumped up as he was.

Chris donned his blaze-orange vest, placed his carefully chosen shells in the loops, put on his orange hat, and we headed for the first covert of the day. (Not only does Michigan have an orange law, kids are so much easier to see that way; they really don't stick up too high in cover.) The sun was drying the frost-killed ferns as Jess locked up at the edge of an old forest road in some thick alder. I placed Chris at the edge of a twenty-yard opening and moved in to flush. A woodcock streaked out ahead of me, low and fast. Chris swung and squeezed the trigger. The bird puffed and Jess made the retrieve. The three of us sat down while one of us smoked his pipe and tried to keep from crying. The deed was done—he's one of us.

The First Season

I exposed Chris to a lot of different forms of hunting that autumn. We hunted woodcock and grouse, ducks, and pheasants. Chris was given the choice shooting position each time for the first month of shooting, and each time we hunted something different. His tally at the end of the year was impressive, but numbers don't tell the story. Being trained properly, Chris didn't get tired, wanted to hunt every day—even in driving rain—and was working me over for a new gun.

About halfway through the season, I gave him an early Christmas present: a little side-by-side straight-gripped 20 Ithaca that weighs five pounds, ten ounces. After school, at the gun club, he got used to the gun, its single trigger, and ejectors. After that, the gun, bored cylinder and improved cylinder (and one of my own favorites up until then) made him blue murder.

The last day of the regular ruffed grouse season, Chris, I, and Jess were joined by my own father for an hour's hunt. In a clearcut on my dad's land, Jess finally nailed a grouse that had been running for a hundred yards. The bird flushed and topped out at twenty-five yards high and fast. From the left, I heard the crack of the boy's 20, and the bird pinwheeled down. I lowered my Parker, broke the gun, and Chris crashed through the brush to me in time to accept the retrieve—his first grouse.

Now he's one of the boys and takes his chances with no special considerations (well, maybe a few). Because of his training, Chris is a better shot than most of the men I hunt with, appreciates nature, autumn colors, and good dog work, and thinks I'm the greatest thing since sliced bread.

If only he'd chip in for gas.

Besides our youngsters coming up, the future is going to hold some other challenges for upland shooters. Among these are places to hunt. In some parts of the United States, leased land is a fact of life, such as in the Southwest, where unless you have a lease or are invited to hunt on one, you simply don't hunt.

Leases are being taken up in other parts of the country as well, especially in those states that have not had a tradition of leasing but offer little public land. There, hunters have had to rely upon the permission of farmers, and many farmers are now giving that permission in exchange for money, either on a daily basis or as seasonal leases to a group of hunters. A lease can run from the cost of the taxes to several dollars an acre for the hunting rights.

Fortunately, public land is available in many of our most populous states, and this land is often managed for a variety of upland species. Part of the future that upland hunters look toward could be brighter with better scouting techniques prior to the time the seasons open, checking out permission, scouting places to hunt, or checking on farming practices that may affect the places we *do* have to hunt.

The number of hunters is dropping in the U. S., yet those who are avid upland hunters will always be with us. We may be headed toward a period similar to that experienced by England and continental Europe, where hunting is enjoyed by only a few and those few are used to paying for their shooting.

For the hunter with an appetite for the shooting life but little time, a shooting preserve makes good sense as an alternative. On a pay-for-sport operation, some for members only, the person is usually charged a flat fee for each bird released; it's then up to him to get the bird. On some places, the fee is in addition to membership dues, which gives the manager some working capital to make the place a little more wild and natural. A good shooting preserve cannot be told from the "real thing," except that the birds are there in numbers beyond what hunters in the 1980s have come to expect.

Another way of ensuring sport is to buy your own land outright, perhaps in concert with a few other shooters, and then manage it for a particular species. There are a number of groups that are willing to give you the advice free on how to get better populations on your land. Among these are The Ruffed Grouse Society, 1400 Lee Drive, Coraopolis, PA 17105; Pheasants Forever, Box 75473, St. Paul, MN, 55175; and Quail Unlimited, Box 10041, Augusta, GA 30903. With some work and a little outlay, you can turn an abandoned farm into an area teeming with wildlife.

But the real future of upland hunting has to be found in the hunters themselves, their ethics and behavior. Every example of poaching, shot-up road signs, ruined crops, and cattle stung with fine shot drives a nail into our collective coffin.

If our sport should end (and I'm optimistic that it won't), the fault isn't going to be in wet springs, posted land, or non-discharge laws. The fault will be in ourselves.